HOW TO
READ
A
WINE LABEL

HOW TO READ A WINE LABEL

Jeffrey M. Pogash

HAWTHORN BOOKS, INC.

PUBLISHERS / NEW YORK

A Howard & Wyndham Company

To my loving parents, who supported me during the writing of this book; to my exceptionally patient and understanding wife, Jocelyne, who assisted me in all revisions; to my dearest grandmother and to the memory of my grandfather.

Contents

PART III
ENJOYING WINES

PART I
CALIFORNIA WINES

Introduction to California Wines

Basically there are three types of wine made in California—generic, varietal, and sparkling wines.

Generic wines are blends of different types of grapes and are given names like BURGUNDY, CHABLIS, RHINE WINE, and SAUTERNE.* These names have been taken from celebrated French and German wine regions in an attempt to give the impression that the California wines using such names capture the general taste of the wines of those regions. The California version, however, should not be looked upon as a duplication of the European wine; it is most often quite different in taste and in quality. When one speaks of a French Chablis, for example, one is talking about a wine that comes from a very specific area of France and that is produced under conditions that have been established by French law. One such condition is that the CHARDONNAY grape (one of the noble grape varieties) must be the only grape used for the production of a Chablis wine. But a California wine labeled "Chablis" is most likely a blend of white wine grapes that are not equal in quality to the Chardonnay. There is no law in California, as there is in France, specifying which grapes are to be used in making a "Cha-

---

*Throughout the book small capital letters have been used to denote terms that are further defined under the appropriate headings.

blis" or a "Burgundy," and in most cases the wineries do not reveal the kinds of grapes they are using for their generic wine.

The ordinary TABLE WINE, sometimes labeled Mountain Red, White Table Wine, or VIN ROSÉ, resembles the generic wines just mentioned, but its producers do not name a European wine region on the label. Sometimes this kind of generic wine is better than the wines with place names on their labels, but this depends upon the integrity of the vintner. The Robert Mondavi winery in Oakville (NAPA VALLEY), California, produces a very nice and inexpensive Red Table Wine and White Table Wine. The red is a blend of some of California's finest grapes, including CABERNET SAUVIGNON, PINOT NOIR, and ZINFANDEL. Mr. Mondavi was one of the first California wine growers to attempt to produce inexpensive, quality generic wines. He was also one of the first to eliminate the practice of naming generic wines after European wine regions. In recent times several other fine wineries have followed suit.

It should be noted that California generic wine (the vin ordinaire of the United States) is, on the whole, far superior to the ordinary table wine consumed by most Frenchmen. In fact, a large quantity of French vin ordinaire is undrinkable, whereas most California generic wines are pleasing to the palate. With this in mind, the American consumer should take advantage of the generic wine bonanza if he or she is in the market for a good (but not great) wine at a relatively low price.

Generic wines should always be less expensive than the second, and most important, type of California wine, the varietal. A varietal wine is named according to the particular grape used to produce it, such as Cabernet Sauvignon, Chardonnay, Pinot Noir, Zinfandel. If a California wine label indicates a grape variety as the name of the wine, then by law that bottle must contain *at least* 51 percent of the grape variety mentioned. In other words, a bottle labeled

THE GREAT STATE OF CALIFORNIA VINEYARDS
Cabernet Sauvignon
Napa Valley, California

must contain at least 51 percent Cabernet Sauvignon. The same percentage holds true for every other varietal wine produced in California.

Some outstanding vineyards use a much higher percentage of the specified grape than the minimum 51 percent. Often this higher percentage will be indicated on a separate label found on the *back* of the bottle. Many California wineries attach this back label to the bottle whether or not they use a high percentage of the varietal grape, and frequently it provides no pertinent information about the wine. An example of a label that gives a great deal of valuable information is the one created by Beaulieu Vineyard. Many BV (Beaulieu Vineyard) varietal wines have the percentage of grapes used to produce the wine written on the back label. Beaulieu Vineyard is noted for this and has been in the forefront of the battle to educate the wine purchaser. We can only hope that more California wineries will adopt the policy that Beaulieu has established.

Some varietal wines are a blend of the juices from two different grapes, the one mentioned on the label being the predominant variety. Other varietal wines contain 100 percent of the specified grape. Even though certain varietals are at their best when they are composed of one type of grape, there are those grapes that yield a better wine when they are blended with another grape variety. Blending two or more different kinds of grapes to produce a varietal wine under one name should not, therefore, be viewed as an attempt to deceive the public. Mixing grape varieties is a common and, if done properly, very legal practice throughout France. In the BORDEAUX region, for example, some of the finest wines are blends of several grapes. The famous CHÂTEAUNEUF-DU-PAPE, from France's RHÔNE VALLEY, sometimes contains a dozen different kinds of grapes.

There are various reasons for blending wine, some of which are unscrupulous. But the reputable California wineries have only the most honorable of intentions when they blend their grapes. If certain grapes were to be used by themselves they would tend to produce wines that might be described as "hard," that is, too tannic (applicable to red wines). Other grapes, if used alone, can cause a wine to be excessively "thin" or lacking in body. But if two or more grapes are used together, they will often produce a smoother and more pleasant wine than would be obtained if only one type of grape were used, provided that the grapes have been blended correctly. Blending the juices from two or more different kinds of grapes to the precise percentages needed to make a fine wine is an art that can only be exercised by the most skillful wine maker. That is why it is important to know which wineries produce the best wines. The following list will provide the names of some of the finer California vineyards whose wines are readily available throughout the United States. I have tried to select those wineries that produce superior varietal wines for about $5.00 the fifth and good generic wines for substantially less.

Almaden Vineyards
Beaulieu Vineyard
Beringer Vineyards
Buena Vista Vineyards
Burgess Cellars
Caymus (or Liberty School)
Chappellet Vineyard (or
    Pritchard Hill)
Chateau St. Jean
Christian Brothers
Concannon Vineyards
Cuvaison
Fetzer Vineyards
Firestone Vineyard
Hoffman Mountain Ranch
    Vineyards (HMR)
Inglenook Vineyards
Kenwood Vineyards
Korbel & Bros.

Charles Krug Winery
Louis M. Martini Winery
Mirassou Vineyards
Robert Mondavi Winery
Oak Hill Winery
Parducci Wine Cellars
J. Pedroncelli Winery
Joseph Phelps
San Martin Winery
Sebastiani Vineyards
Simi Winery
Sonoma Vineyards (or
    Windsor)
Souverain of Rutherford and
    The Alexander Valley
Sterling Vineyards
Sutter Home Winery
Wente Bros.

There are some smaller California wineries whose national distribution may not be as widespread as those just mentioned and whose prices tend to be higher. The wines they produce are usually excellent and many of them are receiving a great deal of recognition from American *and* French wine authorities. These are among the very best wines produced in California today, so if you have the time and the money, do try them.

David Bruce
Callaway Vineyard and Winery
Chalone Vineyard
Chateau Montalena
Clos du Val
Dry Creek Vineyard
Freemark Abbey
Hacienda Wine Cellars
Hanzell Vineyards

Heitz Wine Cellars
Mayacamas Vineyards
Ridge Vineyards
Spring Mountain Vineyards
Stag's Leap Wine Cellars
Stony Hill Vineyard
Joseph Swan
Veedercrest Vineyards
ZD Wines

The higher prices that some of these wineries command can often, but not always, be justified for the following reasons: (1) Drastically smaller quantities of wine are produced, and only a few types of wine are made in contrast with the dozen or two dozen different wines released by many of the larger wineries. (2) The small wineries often plant fewer vines per acre in order to insure a better quality grape. (3) There is usually a longer and/or more carefully watched period of development for the wine. (4) Expensive methods of production are used; for example, the importation of fine European oak barrels for aging. (5) Highly skilled and experienced wine makers are hired by these wineries.

Some of the wineries listed above produce relatively inexpensive varietal wines in addition to their higher-priced wines. Check your wine shop carefully for these bargains.

California is also known for its production of sparkling wines, and the wine purchaser who looks for both quality and good value will certainly turn toward them to satisfy his or her taste for the bubbly. Unfortunately, most wineries have the habit of calling their sparkling wine "Champagne," a most misleading term because California sparkling wine is not the same as French CHAMPAGNE. In some cases, California wineries blend the Pinot Noir and Chardonnay grapes with grapes of lesser quality; other wineries do not even use these noble grapes. In France, only the Pinot Noir, Chardonnay, and Pinot Meunier grapes are allowed in the production of Champagne. But above all, the only place entitled to the Champagne appellation is a specially delimited area within the province of Champagne in France. Even those French wine makers producing sparkling wine in another province, with the same grapes, using exactly the same method, and under the same conditions as in the Champagne region are not legally permitted to call their wine Champagne. For some reason, United States law allows vintners to exploit the name of this great French wine region, and most of them do not hesitate to do so.

California sparkling wine is sometimes an excellent alternative to the often astronomically priced French Champagne. One can find some good examples for less than $7.00, most notably the Brut Champagnes produced by Korbel & Bros. and Hanns Kornell Champagne Cellars. Some of California's best and most expensive sparkling wines are made by Beaulieu Vineyard (Champagne de Chardonnay), Domaine Chandon (Cuvée de Pinot Noir and Napa Valley Brut), Mirassou Vineyards (Au Naturel and Brut), Schramsberg Vineyards (BLANC DE BLANCS and BLANC DE NOIR). These wines are in the $7.00-to-$13.00 price range.

The degree of sweetness in sparkling wine varies from very dry to very sweet, usually in the following order: natural (very dry), brut (dry), extra-dry (slightly sweet), sec or dry (sweet), demi-sec (very sweet).

California Vintages

If a vintage date appears on a wine label it means that at least 95 percent of the grapes used in the wine were harvested in that year. If no vintage date is seen this usually indicates that the wine is a blend of two or more years. A vintage date also requires that at least 95 percent of the volume of the wine be derived from grapes grown within the area mentioned on the label.

The quality of California wine does not vary as much from one year to the next as does the quality of European wine due to the relatively stable climate within the California wine-growing districts. As much as the California wine industry would like us to believe the contrary, it is a fact that California wines can and do vary considerably from year to year. One need only make a side-by-side taste comparison of the same wines from different years in order to discover that it is true. To make a valid statement about the best years for red and white varietal wines, it would be necessary to analyze the California wine region by districts—NAPA,

SONOMA, MENDOCINO, Alameda—or even by microclimates within each district. For simplification, however, I will discuss California vintages in broad terms, hoping the reader will understand that the information may not be consistent for all districts and all types of wine.

The best years for white California varietal wines (especially CHARDONNAY) are 1973, 1974, and 1975. Those years that produced the best red varietal wines (especially CABERNET SAUVIGNON) are 1968, 1969, 1970, 1973, 1975, and 1976.

California Labels

Alcohol   In general, California generic and varietal wines will contain about 12 percent alcohol by volume. The alcoholic content listed on the label may vary by as much as 1½ percent.

Barbera   An Italian grape that yields a very good, full-bodied red wine. The Barbera best accompanies hearty meat and pasta dishes and is often a fine value.

Blanc de Blancs A French expression that means white of whites. In California, any white wine made from any white grape may be labeled "Blanc de Blancs." Some California wineries produce sparkling wine using only the CHARDONNAY grape, as in the CHAMPAGNE region of France (labeled "Champagne de Chardonnay"). Under these circumstances the expression "Blanc de Blancs" is significant; otherwise it is not.

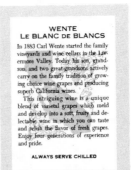

Blanc de Noir   This is a white wine made from black grapes. When the expression is used to refer to a California sparkling wine it may mean that the vintner has attempted to make a wine in the classic CHAMPAGNE style by blending the juice from both black and white grapes. The information provided by the words "Blanc de Noir" concerns the style of the wine rather

than the quality: A sparkling Blanc de Noir will, in most cases, be more full-bodied than a BLANC DE BLANCS, which leans more toward delicacy and lightness. In California, any black grape can produce a Blanc de Noir.

Bottled by   An expression indicating that most of the wine contained in the bottle was produced by some source other than the winery named on the label. Expressions such as "Cellared and bottled by" or "Prepared and bottled by" have the same meaning.

Burgundy   A wine region of France known for its production of outstanding red and white wines made from the PINOT NOIR and CHARDONNAY grapes, respectively. To Americans, Burgundy is most famous for its red wine, so in California the name "Burgundy" refers to a red wine consisting of a blend of several different grapes (in many cases the Pinot Noir is not one of them).

California Burgundy, like other generic wines, comes in half-gallon and gallon jugs, and in the more common 25.6-ounce bottle known as a "fifth." A gallon of Burgundy can usually be purchased for less than $7.00, the half-gallon for less than $4.00, and the fifth for less than $3.00. Since there is no standard blend for wines called Burgundy, their quality will vary considerably from one winery to another.

Cabernet Sauvignon   This is the father of red wine grapes.

It is the noble grape of the BORDEAUX region of France and produces California's most outstanding red wine.

Cabernet grapes tend to make a wine that many inexperienced tasters characterize as "bitter." This bitterness is actually an astringency due to tannin, a substance found in grape skins and wooden casks. A young Cabernet Sauvignon wine often contains a good deal of tannin, making the wine rather unpleasant to drink; but without tannin, the Cabernet Sauvignon could not age into the velvety smooth wine it eventually becomes. Certain California wineries will blend small amounts

of the MERLOT grape with the Cabernet to lessen the astringent quality, and to hasten the aging process. This traditional combination of grapes results in a somewhat lighter and more palatable wine. One should generally allow a Cabernet Sauvignon wine to age in the bottle until it is at least five years old; certain classic bottlings will not become drinkable until they are ten or fifteen years old.

Since the Cabernet Sauvignon grape makes an excellent dry, full-bodied rosé, one might stumble upon a wine label that reads "Cabernet Rosé" or "Rosé of Cabernet Sauvignon." Do try it; the price is usually very reasonable.

EASTERN DISTRIBUTOR "21" Brands, Inc. NEW YORK

12½ % ALCOHOL   BY VOLUME

Vintage of

Special **1969** Selection

California Mountain

CABERNET SAUVIGNON

Produced and Bottled at the Winery by

LOUIS M. MARTINI

ST. HELENA, NAPA COUNTY, CALIFORNIA, U. S. A.

WESTERN DISTRIBUTOR **Parrott & Co.** SAN FRANCISCO

CABERNET SAUVIGNON

This fine, full-bodied red wine is made from grapes of the Cabernet Sauvignon variety, grown within Napa and Sonoma Counties in California.

The Cabernet Sauvignon grape is the variety from which all of the great Clarets (Red Bordeaux) are produced in the Medoc and St. Emilion districts of France, and perhaps more than any other grape it preserves, when transplanted to favorable districts in this country, its unmistakable flavor and bouquet.

This wine should be served at room temperature and is at its best with meats, roasts, fowl and cheese.

The vineyards from which this wine comes are located in the district north of San Francisco, which has been recognized, for nearly a century, as one of the best of this country, for the production of both red and white table wines.

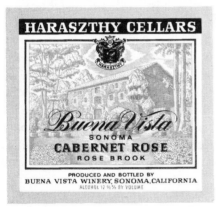

HARASZTHY CELLARS

Buena Vista

SONOMA

CABERNET ROSE

ROSE BROOK

PRODUCED AND BOTTLED BY
BUENA VISTA WINERY, SONOMA, CALIFORNIA
ALCOHOL 12 ½ % BY VOLUME

ROSE BROOK

This wine is from the heritage cellars of Buena Vista, birthplace of fine California wines.

It was here, in 1857, in the fertile golden hillside of Sonoma's Valley of the Moon, that the titled aristocrat of Hungary, Count Agoston Haraszthy, planted the first varietal vines that were to flourish and blossom into today's vast California fine wine industry.

Rose Brook is a very dry pink, or rosé, wine which is somewhat unique from the other types of California rosé in that it is produced almost exclusively from the Cabernet Sauvignon grape which is considered to be the premium claret grape of the world.

All of Buena Vista vineyards are located in California's premium wine growing districts of Napa Valley and Sonoma Valley.

Buena Vista Winery

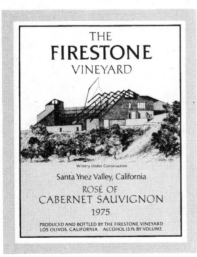

THE

FIRESTONE

VINEYARD

Winery Under Construction

Santa Ynez Valley, California

ROSÉ OF
CABERNET SAUVIGNON
1975

PRODUCED AND BOTTLED BY THE FIRESTONE VINEYARD
LOS OLIVOS, CALIFORNIA   ALCOHOL 13.1% BY VOLUME

This Rosé is made entirely from Cabernet Sauvignon grapes harvested from vineyards in the upper Santa Ynez Valley in early November. The grapes were crushed immediately after picking. The juice was left with the skins for approximately twelve hours before pressing. By taking the juice this quickly from the grape skins, the wine became a deep pink, with a smooth even quality, without the dark, rich overtones of the full skin contact. The wine was fermented slowly at 50 degrees and bottled in early Spring.

This 100% Cabernet Sauvignon wine is complex, yet smooth, the result of the late, cool 1975 harvest from the gravelly soils surrounding the winery, exhibiting an originality of the new region of the Santa Ynez Valley. It is a dry wine, designed to be chilled and enjoyed with light foods. It is a perfect luncheon wine, or would be a beautiful accompaniment to a late brunch.

Brooks Firestone

California   The most important wine-producing region of the United States is unquestionably the state of California, for it is here that some of the very best American wines are found.

The word "California" on a label means that all of the grapes used to produce the wine came from the California wine region and that the wine itself was produced there, e.g., California Cabernet Sauvignon. If the name of a California wine district, such as NAPA VALLEY, SONOMA, MENDOCINO, Alexander Valley, or MONTEREY, appears on a label as part of the name of the wine, as in Napa Valley Chardonnay, this is an indication that at least 75 percent of the grapes used to make the wine came from that area. As a general rule, the more specific an appellation, the more likely it is that the wine will be a good one. Therefore, a wine with a district appellation is often more desirable than a wine with a general California appellation, although this is not always the case. Some California wineries use the name of the vineyard where the grapes were grown on the label, e.g., Martha's Vineyard, Monte Bello, Bosché. A vineyard appellation of this kind is very good because it tells the consumer that all of the grapes came from this one particular area. The use of specific vineyard names on California wine labels is a practice that should be adopted by more wineries.

Carignane   This is not one of California's noble grapes, but the Carignan(e) can yield a hearty red wine with some character.

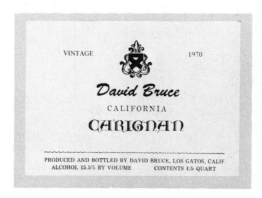

VINTAGE   1970

David Bruce

CALIFORNIA

CARIGNAN

PRODUCED AND BOTTLED BY DAVID BRUCE, LOS GATOS, CALIF.
ALCOHOL 13.5% BY VOLUME   CONTENTS 4/5 QUART

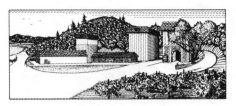

Chablis   A wine district within northern BURGUNDY that produces excellent dry white wines made from the CHARDONNAY grape. California "Chablis" is an ordinary white wine made from a variety of grapes (the Chardonnay is usually not among them). A California Chablis can sometimes be quite sweet even though it is theoretically modeled after the bone-dry French Chablis. Like other generic wines, Chablis is sold in half-gallon and gallon jugs, or in the fifth, and its price is comparable to that of the California Burgundy.

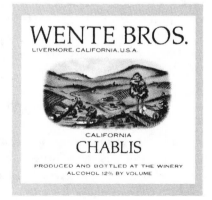

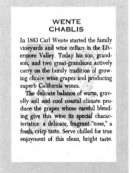

19

NĀPĀ VĀLLEY
CHĀBLIS
ALCOHOL 12½% BY VOLUME
PERFECTED AND BOTTLED IN OUR CELLAR BY
HEITZ WINE CELLĀRS
ST. HELENA, CALIFORNIA

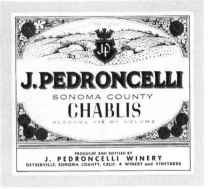

J.PEDRONCELLI
SONOMA COUNTY
CHABLIS
ALCOHOL 12% BY VOLUME

PRODUCED AND BOTTLED BY
J. PEDRONCELLI WINERY
GEYSERVILLE, SONOMA COUNTY, CALIF. ★ WINERY and VINEYARDS

HARASZTHY CELLARS

Buena Vista
SONOMA-NAPA
CHABLIS

PRODUCED AND BOTTLED BY
BUENA VISTA WINERY, SONOMA, CALIFORNIA
ALCOHOL 12 ½% BY VOLUME

CHABLIS

This wine is from the heritage cellars of Buena Vista, birthplace of fine California wines.

It was here, in 1857, in the fertile golden hillside of Sonoma's Valley of the Moon, that the titled aristocrat of Hungary, Count Agoston Haraszthy, planted the first varietal vines that were to flourish and blossom into today's vast California fine wine industry.

Buena Vista Chablis is superb in aroma and flavor. It is a very dry wine, being delicate and mellow to the palate. It is a blend of our fine white varietal wines and is brought into excellent balance through the skill and experience of our winemaster.

All of Buena Vista vineyards are located in California's premium wine growing districts of Napa Valley and Sonoma Valley.

Buena Vista Winery

Champagne   Though true Champagne can only be made within the delimited area of France known as Champagne, California wineries still insist upon usurping the name for their sparkling wines. Federal law states, however, that all wineries using the name "Champagne" on a label must place the name of the wine's true place of origin before the word "Champagne." California wineries producing this type of sparkling wine must call their product California Champagne, and not just Champagne. If at least 75 percent of the grapes used to produce the wine come from some geographical subdivision of California like the NAPA VALLEY, a winery is then entitled to use the name of that area on the label preceding the word "Champagne"—for example, Napa Valley Champagne.

20

Champagne Method (or MÉTHODE CHAMPENOISE) The

finest sparkling wines are made by the method that has been
used in the province of Champagne since the seventeenth century. The *Méthode Champenoise* consists in allowing the already fermented still (nonsparkling) wine to ferment a second
time in individual bottles so that it may become effervescent.
These wines made in the classic manner of the Champagne region will carry such expressions as "Naturally fermented in
this bottle" or "Produced by the Champagne Method" on the
label.

Another method frequently used in California to make
sparkling wine is called the Transfer Process. It is like the traditional Champagne method in that the still wine is fermented
in the bottle to obtain the sparkle. Unlike the Champagne
method, however, the wine is transferred from the bottle to
storage tanks for filtering after it has undergone its second fermentation. During this process the wine is stored in such a
way as to allow it to retain its sparkle. Sparkling wines that
have been made according to the Transfer method will usually
have the expression "Naturally fermented in the bottle" written on the label. This method has been used with a good deal
of success in California, producing some very fine sparkling
wines.

Cheaper sparkling wines are made according to the Bulk (or
Charmat) process of fermentation whereby a large quantity of
wine is fermented in glass tanks and then bottled after it has
become sparkling. This procedure requires much less time,
care, and money than does either the traditional Champagne

method or the Transfer process. Those sparkling wines made according to the Bulk process must be labeled "Bulk Process" or "Charmat Process."

Chardonnay (or PINOT CHARDONNAY)   This is the best white wine grape of both France and California. It produces a very dry white wine with much character and delicacy. In BUR-GUNDY, the Chardonnay grape is responsible for the CHABLIS and the great MONTRACHETS. In CHAMPAGNE, it is used in conjunction with the PINOT NOIR grape to create the delightful sparkling wines of that region.

Some California wineries believe in aging the juice from the Chardonnay grape in oak barrels for a lengthy period of time so that it picks up the flavor of the wood. Such a wine is often

superb and is given an added dimension of complexity during this process because of a "vanilla" flavor that is imparted to the wine by the oak. Other wineries prefer not to give their Chardonnay wines a strong oaklike quality. The back label will sometimes lend a clue as to the oakiness of the wine, but your own experiences with particular California wineries will ultimately provide you with the best information concerning those qualities you enjoy most in the Chardonnay.

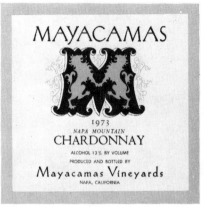

Chenin Blanc   A white wine grape that has been dubbed "Pineau de la Loire" because it thrives in France's famed LOIRE VALLEY. Depending upon weather conditions and the particular style that is desired, the Chenin Blanc grape produces wines ranging from very dry to sweet. California Chenin Blanc wines are often very good values.

The name "Chenin Blanc" is most likely to be seen on a California wine label, but it is also possible to find Pineau de la Loire or WHITE PINOT as names for the same wine.

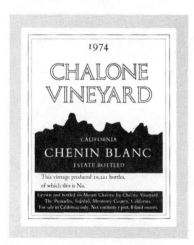

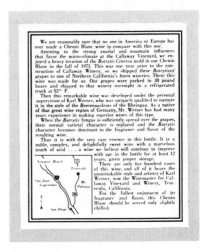

Chianti Once again we have an example of an attempt to imitate another country's wine, in this case Italy. Since there are no laws regulating which grapes are to be used in a California "Chianti," the wine maker is free to produce his wine from just about any grape he can find. A California Chianti will be red, like the original Italian version, but who knows what it will taste like?

Claret   This is a word used more frequently in England than in the United States, so wine enthusiasts will rarely see it on a California label. "Claret" has become synonymous with "Red Table Wine"; it is the English adaptation of the word "clairet," which means a light red wine with little color. While the BORDEAUX region of France was under English rule (beginning in the twelfth century), the word "claret" found its way into our language and has remained there ever since. As is the case with other generic wines, a Claret will be a blend of lesser grapes—it will always be red.

12½% ALCOHOL   BY VOLUME

California Mountain
CLARET
Prepared and Bottled at the Winery by
LOUIS M. MARTINI
ST. HELENA, NAPA COUNTY, CALIFORNIA, U.S.A.

Emerald Riesling
This California hybrid is a cross between the JOHANNISBERG RIESLING and the MUSCADELLE grapes. The result is a very interesting white wine with flowery and spicy characteristics. The Emerald Riesling is often a very good value.

LIMITED 1975 VINTAGE

SanMartin
SINCE 1892

SANTA CLARA VALLEY

Emerald Riesling

This unique white wine is light, crisp and fruity in taste. There is a clean, summer freshness to its bouquet and a jewel-like brilliance to its pale, greenish straw color. Produced and bottled by San Martin Vineyards Company, San Martin, California. Alcohol 11 percent by volume

SanMartin
1975 Vintage
Emerald Riesling

The Emerald Riesling is a truly unique varietal grape developed in California from the classic Johannisberg Riesling and the Muscat de Alexandria. San Martin's Emerald Riesling, with its crisp fruitiness, comes from 32 acres of these varietal grapes at our San Ysidro Vineyards within California's Northcoast, Santa Clara Valley. A light fragrant wine, it is chilled during fermentation to hold its youth. After filtering to gain brilliance, it is allowed to settle before blending by our winemaster for the highest varietal characteristics. Once bottled and allowed another brief rest, this young, joyous wine is ready for its debut. San Martin Vineyards has been a producer of fine California wines since 1892.

Serve slightly chilled.

Estate Bottled
The Estate Bottled designation indicates that the entire wine-making process took place on property owned or controlled by the winery named on the label. Many California wineries buy grapes from independent growers and then proceed to make wine. But an estate-bottled wine has been produced from start to finish by the named winery, including the growing of the grapes.

The quality of a wine cannot be guaranteed merely because the label carries the words "Estate Bottled," for the term is not very significant as it is now defined.

28

Folle Blanche Traditionally, a blending grape for white generic wines. The Folle Blanche is widely planted in France but produces only a mediocre dry white wine there as in California.

French Colombard Like the FOLLE BLANCHE, the Colombard grape is used extensively in the blending of white generic and some sparkling wines. French Colombard is an inexpensive dry white wine of fair quality.

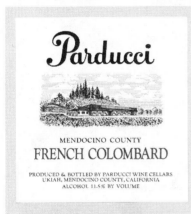

Fumé Blanc (see SAUVIGNON BLANC)

Gamay (or NAPA GAMAY) This is the grape that is used to make BEAUJOLAIS in France, but it does not have the same success in California. The red and rosé wines that the Gamay grape produces are at times good, but quality varies depending upon the winery.

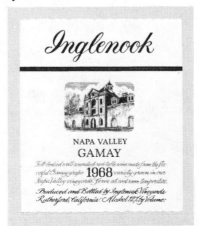

29

Gamay Beaujolais   The Gamay Beaujolais grape of California is thought to be a relative of the PINOT NOIR grape, and not the GAMAY. It produces red and rosé wines of good quality.

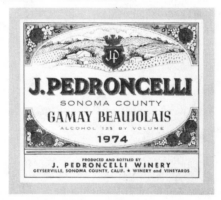

Gewurztraminer   The Traminer grape is responsible for one of California's most interesting white wines. When at its best, it yields a spicy and flowery wine called Gewurztraminer (Spicy Traminer). Unfortunately, most California Gewurztraminers do not possess the same originality and distinction as their Alsatian counterparts, but they are well worth sampling just the same.

A LATE HARVEST Gewurztraminer will probably have an even greater spicy and perfumed character (and an added touch of sweetness) due to the use of very ripe grapes. The words "Late Harvest" will appear on the front label of such a wine.

A Selected Bottling of
California.

Gewürztraminer

Vintage 1972

Produced from grapes grown
on our Arroyo Seco Vineyards
and bottled by

Wente Bros.

Livermore, California
Alcohol, 12% by volume

STONY HILL

NAPA VALLEY

GEWÜRZ TRAMINER

1974

Grown, produced and bottled 600 feet
above the floor of the Napa Valley by
Stony Hill Vineyard, St. Helena, Calif.

ALCOHOL 12.5% BY VOLUME

Dry Creek

1975

Alexander Valley

GEWÜRZTRAMINER

This vintage produced
3700 bottles   Alcohol 13% by volume

PRODUCED AND BOTTLED BY
DRY CREEK VINEYARD, HEALDSBURG, CALIFORNIA

Vineyard

GEWÜRZTRAMINER

The Gewürztraminer grape, of Alsatian origin, has begun to be recognized as producing superior quality wines when planted in the right location. The Alexander Valley of Sonoma County seems to be one of these favored areas. This wine is made from Gewürztraminer grown by Redwood Ranch and Vineyard in the Alexander Valley. Harvested on September 20 and 22, 1975, at a sugar content of 23.0° Brix and a total acidity of 0.67, the wine was cold fermented to about 1% sugar at which time the fermentation was stopped by refrigeration, thus leaving a slight amount of residual sugar. Bottling occurred in April 1976.

We are very pleased with our initial Gewürztraminer and invite you to try this and our other Dry Creek Vineyard wines.

David S. Stare
Winemaker
DRY CREEK VINEYARD, HEALDSBURG, CALIFORNIA

VINEYARDS ESTABLISHED 1825

Sebastiani

FOUNDED AT THE END OF EL CAMINO REAL

SONOMA

GEWÜRZ TRAMINER

Soft and Spicy

PRODUCED AND BOTTLED BY SEBASTIANI VINEYARDS
SONOMA VALLEY, CALIFORNIA
ALC. 12% BY VOL. BONDED WINERY 876

VINEYARDS ESTABLISHED 1825

Sebastiani

GEWÜRZ TRAMINER

The Sebastiani Gewürz Traminer is a varietal wine made largely of the Gewürz Traminer grape with other carefully selected varieties blended in to add to the overall character.

After careful fermentation in a temperature controlled stainless steel tank the wine is aged for several months, bottled, bottle-aged, and released at its delicate and spicy best.

This delightful wine should be served moderately chilled with delicate courses of fish, seafood, fowl and other light foods.

SINCE 1825

Our heritage started in Sonoma, the end of El Camino Real, in 1825 and Shine Cellars (Historical Landmark No. 739) marks the location. One of the few remaining family wineries in California, we desire the name Sebastiani be associated only with quality.

Your enjoyment and approval of this selection is the reward of our family effort.

Green Hungarian An ordinary white wine grape used principally in generic wines. Some wineries do bottle Green Hungarian as a varietal wine.

Grenache This grape produces a superior rosé in California and in France. A California Grenache Rosé is rich in color, very fruity, and sometimes has a pleasant touch of sweetness. If you are a rosé fan (and even if you are not), the California Grenache Rosé is the one to buy when looking for a nice drinkable wine to accompany a simple meal. It is usually available for less than $4.00.

Beaulieu
Vineyard

BV

CALIFORNIA
GRENACHE ROSÉ
A LIGHT WINE OF GRENACHE GRAPES

PRODUCED & BOTTLED BY BEAULIEU VINEYARD
AT RUTHERFORD, NAPA COUNTY, CALIFORNIA

ALCOHOL 12.5% BY VOLUME

Beaulieu **BV** Vineyard
CALIFORNIA
GRENACHE ROSÉ

**Produced entirely from
Grenache Grapes**

THE rosé wine from the Grenache grape of
Southern France, responsible for the well known
Tavel, has found a hearty welcome in this country.
BV Grenache Rosé, made from selected grapes of
this variety, possesses the fine quality traditional
with Beaulieu Vineyard.

The French call rosé "vin d'une nuit"—wine of
one night. It comes from red wine grapes, but for
rosé the juice is left with the skins only a few
hours after the crushing, thus acquiring no more
than a touch of their natural color.

This fresh, pleasant wine goes well with every
food. Its pale ruby clarity, full fragrance and fruity
flavor lend a festive air to any meal, from picnic to
dinner party. It is best served chilled.

Sonoma Vineyards
California
Grenache Rosé
1973

PRODUCED AND BOTTLED AT THE WINERY BY SONOMA VINEYARDS
WINDSOR, SONOMA COUNTY, CALIFORNIA, ALCOHOL 12% BY VOLUME

HMR
California
GRENACHE
ROSÉ

Hoffman Mountain Ranch
Vineyards

Santa Lucia Mountains, Paso Robles, California
Alcohol 13.5% by Volume

Vineyards Established 1852

Serve   Chilled

ALMADÉN
California
GRENACHE ROSÉ

A fresh, appetizing fragrant rosé wine made
from the famous Grenache grape of France, grown in
the fine wine vineyards of Northern California.

MADE AND BOTTLED BY
Almadén Vineyards, Los Gatos, California
Alcohol 12½% by volume

ALMADÉN GRENACHE ROSÉ

This delightful pink or rosé wine, fresh and fragrant
as a spring garden, was the first vin rosé to be produced
in commercial quantities in this country, and is now
the most popular such wine. Dry, yet fruity, light, attractive, it goes well with almost any dish; it should
be served very cold.

The Grenache grape is widely grown in Europe,
especially in Southern France, where it yields the
celebrated vin rosé of Tavel; considered the best of all
grapes for rosé, it gives, in the cooler districts of California, a wine as good as any rosé in the world.

The vineyards from which it comes are in the heart
of one of America's great wine districts—the fine wine
vineyards of Northern California. Here the cool nights
and warm days enable the grapes to reach perfection.
Climate, soil and exposure are at their best, remarkably like those of the famous wine lands of Europe.

Grey Riesling   The Grey is not a member of the RIESLING family of grapes, nor does it possess the qualities of a noble grape like the JOHANNISBERG RIESLING—the only true Riesling in California. The Grey is white and dry (like the real thing) and inexpensive.

Johannisberg Riesling   This is the true RIESLING grape found in France and Germany. The delicate and subtle white wine that comes from the Johannisberg Riesling grape is one of California's truly superior varietal wines. The Johannisberg Riesling is a noble grape, so do not be fooled by other ignoble imitators that call themselves Riesling, like GREY RIESLING, EMERALD RIESLING, or the simple RIESLING (made from the SYLVANER grape). The Johannisberg Riesling grape also goes by the name of WHITE RIESLING in California.

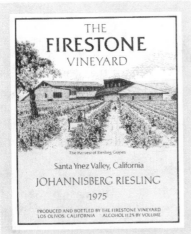

THE
FIRESTONE
VINEYARD

The Harvest of Riesling Grapes

Santa Ynez Valley, California

JOHANNISBERG RIESLING

1975

PRODUCED AND BOTTLED BY THE FIRESTONE VINEYARD
LOS OLIVOS, CALIFORNIA · ALCOHOL 11.2% BY VOLUME

The grapes used to produce this White, or Johannisberg Riesling, came from four White Riesling vineyards within one half mile of the Winery, harvested in mid-October. Everyone who picked these grapes enjoyed their flavor, and the crush and press area held a beautiful aroma.

The grapes experienced a beneficial degree of Botrytis, or "Noble Rot." After immediate pressing, the juice was fermented slowly at 50 degrees and after fermentation, aged for a short period in oak.

The development of this Riesling was designed to retain a slightly sweet character, reminiscent of a German Mosel, balanced by an inherent dry, chalky or flint-like quality derived from the local soil.

This is our first harvest and our first white wine to be released. It is the first Riesling to be produced from grapes grown exclusively in the Santa Ynez Valley.

Brooks Firestone

1975

Chateau St. Jean

MENDOCINO COUNTY

Johannisberg Riesling

Late Harvest

MARCH VINEYARDS

PRODUCED AND BOTTLED BY
CHATEAU ST. JEAN · KENWOOD, SONOMA VALLEY, CALIFORNIA
BONDED WINERY NO. 4710 · ALCOHOL 10.5% BY VOLUME

CHATEAU
MONTELENA

ESTABLISHED 1882

Late Harvest NAPA & ALEXANDER VALLEYS

Johannisberg Riesling

1974

PRODUCED AND BOTTLED BY CHATEAU MONTELENA WINERY
CALISTOGA, NAPA VALLEY, CALIFORNIA · ALCOHOL 10.5% BY VOLUME

CALLAWAY
Vineyard & Winery

Estate Bottled
Vintage 1974

TEMECULA, CALIFORNIA

White Riesling

Grown, Vinified and Bottled by Callaway Vineyard & Winery
Temecula, California · Alcohol 11.9% By Volume

Callaway Vineyard and Winery is small and privately owned, located 1400' high on a hilltop in California's south coast mountain region, 23 miles from the Pacific Ocean.

Callaway Vineyard has well drained, highly granitic soil and a unique micro-climate very favorable for the six premium varietal wines we grow. A strong coastal influence brings cooling breezes and mist to moderate the clear summer days, and chill the moist nights.

Winemaster Karl Werner is internationally recognized for making superior wines in his native Germany and in California. He insists we keep our grape yield very low; hand harvest them only when fully and properly mature; then rush them into our winery within 70 minutes. There the grapes are de-stemmed prior to crushing and pressing in ultra modern equipment made for us in France and Germany. Callaway wines are then allowed to develop slowly . . . using the best of traditional practices found only at certain small, fine wine estates in Europe and America.

Callaway's White Riesling (Johannisberg) is dry . . . with less than 6/10th of 1% residual sugar.

After controlled fermentation lasting at least 12 weeks, this 1974 wine was matured lightly in oval casks made from selected German white oak coopered in Germany especially for us. The wine was made in the style of the great White Riesling of the Rheingau. Given proper storage, it should continue to improve in the bottle for at least six years.

Callaway wines are unique . . . with their own distinct character in aroma, bouquet, color and flavor. Each wine contains at least 95% the grape varietal designated.

For fullest enjoyment of its fragrance and flavor, our White Riesling should be served only moderately chilled.

Late Harvest   The term "Late Harvest" is sometimes seen on California wine labels, especially in connection with the Johannisberg Riesling grape. It indicates that the grapes used to make the wine were picked after the normal harvest and were, therefore, very ripe. A Late Harvest wine is richer, sweeter, and more full bodied than wine made from grapes harvested at the usual time. Late Harvest wines are usually more expensive than regular bottlings.

Livermore   A wine-producing district southeast of San Francisco known especially for its fine white wines. There are several excellent wineries in the Livermore Valley, including Concannon and Wente Bros.

Made and Bottled by   Indicates that at least 10 percent of the wine was actually produced by the winery named on the label.

Malbec   Vintners in the BORDEAUX region of France often blend the Malbec grape with the CABERNET SAUVIGNON in order to help their red wines mature more rapidly. The use of Malbec is not as widespread in California as it is in France, but occasionally one might see it listed on the back label of a bottle of Cabernet Sauvignon. California wineries do not, at present, bottle Malbec under its own varietal name.

Mendocino   Some very good varietal and generic wines have come from this northern wine district, but Mendocino is still in

the early stages of its development. Fetzer Vineyards and Parducci Wine Cellars produce some of the best wines in Mendocino county.

Merlot   In California, the Merlot has been used primarily as a
blending grape for CABERNET SAUVIGNON, but within recent
years a few wineries like Louis M. Martini and Sterling have

STERLING
VINEYARDS

Napa Valley
MERLOT
Grown, Produced and Bottled by Sterling Vineyards,
Calistoga-Napa Valley-California
alcohol 12½ % by volume

12½% ALCOHOL   BY VOLUME

Vintage of
1973

California Mountain

MERLOT

Produced and Bottled at the Winery by
LOUIS M. MARTINI
ST. HELENA, NAPA COUNTY, CALIFORNIA

MERLOT

This fine medium bodied red wine is made from grapes of the Merlot variety, grown within Napa and Sonoma Counties in California.

The Merlot grape is the variety most often blended with the Cabernet Sauvignon to produce the great Bordeaux wines of the Medoc, St. Emilion and Pomerol districts of France. In Northern Italy and Switzerland it produces a varietal wine of excellent quality. It is reminiscent of a Cabernet Sauvignon but is softer and matures more quickly.

This wine should be served at room temperature and is at its best with meats, roasts, fowl and cheese.

The vineyards from which this wine comes are located in the districts north of San Francisco, which have been recognized, for over a century, as one of the best of this country for the production of both red and white table wines.

begun bottling Merlot as a varietal wine. The Merlot grape produces a very mellow, full-bodied red wine that is excellent for those people who don't usually care for red wine.

Méthode Champenoise (see CHAMPAGNE METHOD)

Monterey   Located to the south of San Francisco, this county has not yet realized its full wine-producing potential. Several wineries have planted both red and white wine grapes in Monterey, and they appear to be doing quite well, especially the white grapes. The Mirassou and Wente Wineries are having

great success here, particularly with the JOHANNISBERG RIESLING and GEWURZTRAMINER grape varieties. The future looks bright for the vineyards of Monterey county.

WENTE
JOHANNISBERG RIESLING

In 1883 Carl Wente started the family vineyards and wine cellars in the Livermore Valley. Today his son, grandson, and two great-grandsons actively carry on the family tradition of growing choice wine grapes and producing superb California wines.

The grapes that produce this flowery White (Johannisberg) Riesling are grown in Monterey County. The unique climate and soil of the Arroyo Seco vineyards produce a most distinctive Riesling with a fine fruity acidity that is at its best at a relatively early age.

Mountain   This term is very popular with California wineries, but it is also rather confusing to a great many consumers. The word "Mountain" has no legal significance, whether it is applied to generic or varietal wines. The actual meaning of the term depends upon the individual winery. Sometimes "Mountain" may mean that the wine is lighter than the others produced by that winery. At other times it might indicate that the grapes used in the wine were grown on or near a mountain. One thing is certain, the term "Mountain" does not imply quality.

Muscadelle

The Muscadelle grape is respected in France because it is blended in small quantities with the SAUVIGNON BLANC and the SEMILLON to produce the exquisite dessert wine known as SAUTERNES. Some California wineries make similar Sauternes-style blends, using the Muscadelle grape for added aroma and flavor. The Muscadelle is not bottled as a varietal wine, but one will sometimes see the name on back labels. The EMERALD RIESLING grape is a cross between the Muscadelle and the JOHANNISBERG RIESLING grapes.

Napa

The Napa Valley, northeast of San Francisco, is probably the most prestigious wine district in the United States, for it is here that most of our truly great American wines are made. To the delight of Napa wine growers the valley is blessed with the proper natural elements (soil and climate) that

enable both red and white grapes to thrive. The CABERNET SAU-
VIGNON, CHARDONNAY, and JOHANNISBERG RIESLING (all noble
grapes of France) often yield superb wines in the Napa area, as
do some of the other fine European grapes that are grown
there.

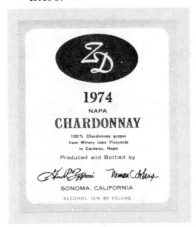 

Napa Gamay (see GAMAY)

North Coast Counties
Wines with a North Coast Coun-
ties appellation are made from grapes that come from several
counties in the San Francisco area known for their cool cli-
mates, the most important of which are Alameda, MENDOCINO,
MONTEREY, NAPA, SONOMA, and Santa Clara. Since the North
Coast Counties encompass a very large area, this appellation
is not as significant as a more specific appellation such as Mendocino or Sonoma.

41

1975

Chateau St. Jean

NORTH COAST COUNTIES

Chardonnay

PRODUCED AND BOTTLED BY
CHATEAU ST. JEAN · KENWOOD, SONOMA VALLEY, CALIFORNIA
BONDED WINERY NO 4710 · ALCOHOL 13.2% BY VOLUME

Petite Sirah   The Concannon Vineyards first introduced this wine as a varietal sixteen years ago when few people had ever heard of it. Today, Petite Sirah is bottled by some two dozen California wineries and is becoming very popular with wine lovers. When young, the Petite Sirah grape yields a fruity and spicy red wine that is high in tannin. In time (about five years or so) this wine can become quite smooth and pleasant. The Petite Sirah grape of California should not be confused with the noble Syrah of the Rhone valley, for they are not the same.

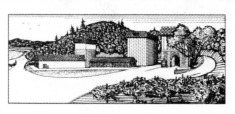

1973 PETITE SYRAH

This full-bodied and flavorful wine is made 100% from Petite Syrah grown in two carefully selected vineyards located in Mendocino County, California.

The grapes were delivered to our winery in mid October 1973 at over 22% Brix. After a long fermentation the wine was aged in small casks. It was bottled at our winery in the spring of 1975.

Fetzer

1973

MENDOCINO

PETITE SYRAH

PRODUCED AND BOTTLED BY

Fetzer Vineyards

REDWOOD VALLEY, CALIFORNIA
ALCOHOL 12% BY VOLUME

John E. Fetzer

FETZER VINEYARDS

Pinot Blanc The white wine made from the Pinot Blanc grape is very dry and has good varietal character. It is an enjoyable wine and is usually priced at less that $4.00. WHITE PINOT (the correct English translation of Pinot Blanc) is another name for the CHENIN BLANC grape, *not* for the Pinot Blanc.

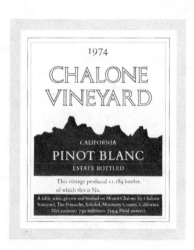

Pinot Chardonnay (see CHARDONNAY)

Pinot Noir   This is the noble red wine grape of BURGUNDY that has met with limited success in California. There are some fine examples of California Pinot Noir, but not many. Chalone Vineyard, Hanzell Vineyard, Heitz Cellars, and ZD Wines make some of the best Pinot Noir in California. Other good examples come from Beaulieu Vineyard, Louis M. Martini, Parducci Wine Cellars, and the Robert Mondavi Winery. Some dry white Pinot Noir is also made by a few wineries.

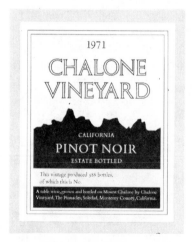

1969
Napa Valley
PINOT NOIR
ALCOHOL 13% BY VOLUME
PRODUCED AND BOTTLED BY
ROBERT MONDAVI WINERY
OAKVILLE, CALIFORNIA

12½ % ALCOHOL   BY VOLUME

Special *Vintage of* 1969 Selection

California Mountain

PINOT NOIR

Produced and Bottled at the Winery by

LOUIS M. MARTINI

ST. HELENA, NAPA COUNTY, CALIFORNIA, U.S.A.

MOUNTAIN PINOT NOIR

This fine, full-bodied, dry red wine is made from grapes of the celebrated Pinot Noir variety, grown within Napa and Sonoma Counties in California. Delicate yet possessing the authority which the true Pinot grape imparts, it is at its best with red meat, roasts, steaks, game or cheese. It should be served at room temperature or, in hot weather, at cellar temperature if desired.

The yield per acre from Pinot Noir grapes is very low, and a genuine Pinot is never inexpensive. Essentially the Pinot Noir is a cool country grape, and the few small plantings that exist in this country are in the North Coast Counties of California.

The vineyards from which this wine comes are located in the district north of San Francisco, which has been recognized, for nearly a century, as one of the best of this country, for the production of both red and white table wines.

ZD

1970

NAPA

PINOT NOIR

100% Pinot Noir grapes
from Carneros, Napa

Produced and Bottled by

SONOMA, CALIFORNIA

ALCOHOL 12% BY VOLUME

PINOT NOIR

The wine in this bottle has been produced entirely from Pinot Noir grapes grown in the Carneros region at the southern tip of Napa County. The climate in this region is ideal for growing grapes which result in wines of full varietal character. As the vines increase in maturity, the wines produced from the grapes develop a rich flavor which was exceptionally evident during the remarkable 1970 vintage.

The grapes were picked from a select hillside vineyard on September 8, 1970, at a sugar content of 23.9° balling and a total acidity of .89 gm/100ml. After crushing and stemming, the must was allowed to ferment 4 days in a redwood vat. The wine was then separated from the grape skins and fermented to complete dryness in 50 gallon barrels. By allowing a natural malolactic fermentation to occur and aging partly in American oak and partly in limousin oak, the wine flavor acquired a touch of oak and complexity.

The wine was bottled in February, 1973. It is full bodied and extremely Pinot Noir in character. It has excellent aging qualities and should be bottle aged at least a few years before being consumed.

This wine is natural and unfined, and during aging is expected to produce a slight sediment.

P. O. Box 900   Sonoma, Calif. 95476

Pinot St. Georges (also called Red Pinot) A red wine grape that is not of the true Pinot strain. It yields a fruity but undistinguished wine.

Rhine Wine   A California Rhine Wine is white and is often, but not always, on the sweet side. It will probably not bear any resemblance to a true German wine, so don't be disappointed.

Riesling This name has been responsible for an inordinate amount of confusion. There are wines called GREY RIESLING, EMERALD RIESLING, SYLVANER RIESLING, and JOHANNISBERG RIESLING (the only pure Riesling of the lot). California wine labels that bear the name "Riesling" or "Sylvaner Riesling" designate wines made from the Sylvaner, a perfectly respectable grape, but *not* a Riesling.

The noble Riesling grape, long associated with the outstanding white wines of ALSACE France and of Germany, is called the Johannisberg Riesling in California.

Rosé (or VIN ROSÉ) There are some very good rosés produced in California, but the best are made from the GRENACHE or CABERNET SAUVIGNON grapes and are labeled as such. A label with the words "Rosé" or "Vin Rosé," without any indication of a particular grape variety, is an ordinary generic wine.

Ruby Cabernet This California hybrid is a cross between the CABERNET SAUVIGNON and the CARIGNANE grapes. The rather unusual marriage did not result in a particularly noteworthy offspring.

Sauterne(s) To add insult to injury, California wineries have seen fit to change the French spelling of SAUTERNES by dropping the final *s*. Well, if they can so drastically change the composition of the French wine, I imagine they can and perhaps should drop the last letter of the name. California "Sauterne," an or-

dinary generic white wine, is most often not made from the same grapes as French Sauternes and will probably be a rather dry wine, in contrast with the lusciously sweet and rich French Sauternes.

Sauvignon Blanc

Also known as the FUMÉ BLANC (or Blanc Fumé), the Sauvignon Blanc grape produces one of the finest dry white wines of California. Unfortunately, California Sauvignon Blanc has not received the full attention it deserves from consumers. It is a fine original wine with a slightly "smoky" flavor and usually sells for less than $5.00, making it a good value.

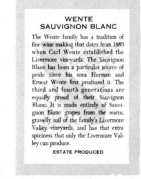

1974
Napa Valley
FUMÉ BLANC
Dry Sauvignon Blanc
ALCOHOL 12% BY VOLUME
PRODUCED AND BOTTLED BY
ROBERT MONDAVI WINERY
OAKVILLE, CALIFORNIA

Semillon   Together with the SAUVIGNON BLANC and the MUSCA-
DELLE, the Semillon helps to produce the dessert wines of SAU-
TERNES. Some California wineries make sweet white wines
using this traditional Sauternes blend, but the Semillon grape
is most often used to make a dry white wine of considerable
flavor that is generally labeled "Dry Semillon" in California.

VINTAGE 1975
Concannon
vineyard
SINCE 1883
ESTATE BOTTLED
LIVERMORE VALLEY
SEMILLON
ALCOHOL 12% BY VOLUME
PRODUCED AND BOTTLED BY
CONCANNON VINEYARD
LIVERMORE, CALIFORNIA

Charles Krug
NAPA VALLEY
DRY SEMILLON
PRODUCED AND BOTTLED BY
Charles Krug Winery
ST. HELENA · CALIFORNIA
ALCOHOL 12% BY VOLUME

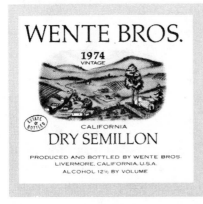

WENTE BROS.
1974
VINTAGE
CALIFORNIA
DRY SEMILLON
PRODUCED AND BOTTLED BY WENTE BROS.
LIVERMORE, CALIFORNIA, U.S.A.
ALCOHOL 12% BY VOLUME

WENTE
DRY SEMILLON
In 1883 Carl Wente started the family
vineyards and wine cellars in the Livermore Valley. Today his son, grandson, and two great-grandsons actively
carry on the family tradition of growing choice wine grapes and producing
superb California wines.
   This wine is made from the exceptional Semillon grape, which grows
particularly well in the warm and gravelly soil of the Livermore Valley. When
carefully aged in the Wente Cellars,
this Dry Semillon develops its full,
aromatic flavor and bouquet.

ESTATE PRODUCED

Sonoma   The two most impressive wine districts of California are NAPA and Sonoma. Like the Napa Valley, Sonoma produces excellent red and white wines. The Alexander and Russian River valleys, two good grape-growing areas, are located in Sonoma county. Some of the better wineries of Sonoma include Buena Vista Vineyards, Dry Creek Vineyard, Hacienda Wine Cellars, Hanzell Vineyards, Kenwood Vineyards, J. Pedroncelli Winery, Simi Winery, Sonoma Vineyards (Windsor), and ZD Wines.

Sylvaner   The white wine grape most often used in California wines calling themselves RIESLING is the Sylvaner. Unfortunately, the Sylvaner does not possess the finesse of the true Riesling grape and should not be thought of as its equal. The wine made from the Sylvaner grape is light and fruity but is sometimes lacking in body. Remember that in California only wines labeled "Johannisberg Riesling" (or "White Riesling") are made from the true European Riesling grape.

Table Wine   Any still (nonsparkling) wine that contains between 10 and 14 percent alcohol by volume. A wine labeled "Red Table Wine" or "White Table Wine" is in the generic wine family. The term "Light Wine" is sometimes used on a label in place of the term "Table Wine."

Vin Rosé (see ROSÉ)

White Pinot (see CHENIN BLANC)

White Riesling (see JOHANNISBERG RIESLING)

Zinfandel   Although this grape originally came from Europe (its country of origin is still unknown), it has certainly found a home in California, for it is there that Zinfandel thrives.
   The Zinfandel is capable of producing a light and fruity red wine that resembles French BEAUJOLAIS, or a more full-bodied and richer wine that is somewhat similar to CABERNET SAUVIGNON. Some of the best Zinfandel wines have a very distinctive "berry" taste and are quite enjoyable either by themselves or

as an accompaniment to a fine meal. Zinfandel is interesting because of its unique varietal characteristics *and* its relatively low price; there are some fine bottles of this wine available for less than $4.00. The richer and more elegant examples of Zinfandel have higher price tags. A limited amount of white Zinfandel is also available.

ZINFANDEL   1968 BOTTLED 7/70. This is **not** a "claret" (light-red) type of Zinfandel. Handle it carefully, for it is so deeply pigmented that shaking up the sediment makes it almost opaque. Aside from that, we leave you room to write your own description. In one word, my own might be SURPRISE.   DRB (3/71)

RIDGE wine is made with an emphasis on quality and naturalness that is rarely attempted. Our grapes are grown in select vineyards (our own except for Zinfandel), where they are left to ripen to peak maturity, often at some loss of quantity. We let the wine settle and age in small barrels, with only rare cellar treatment other than racking. Varieties are not blended unless so indicated on the label. Near Black Mountain on Monte Bello Ridge, our main vineyard is 10 miles south of Palo Alto, 15 miles inland from the ocean, and over 2000 feet in elevation. For requesting an appointment, please send a note by mail or leave a phone message regarding your interests at (408) 867-3233 or (415) 322-2685.

RIDGE
CALIFORNIA
ZINFANDEL

1968

JIMSOMARE VINEYARD 1500' MONTE BELLO RIDGE BOTTLED JULY 1970 ALCOHOL 15%   BY VOLUME PRODUCED AND BOTTLED BY RIDGE VINEYARDS 17100 MONTE BELLO RD, CUPERTINO, CALIFORNIA

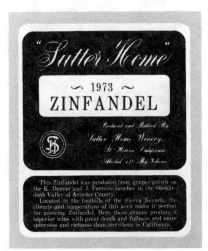

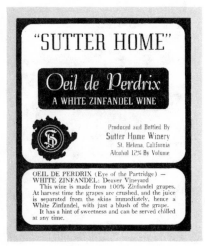

fetzeR

1974

MENDOCINO
RICETTI
ZINFANDEL

PRODUCED AND BOTTLED BY

fetzeR VineyaRÒs

REDWOOD VALLEY, CALIFORNIA
ALCOHOL 12% BY VOLUME

RICETTI ZINFANDEL

The Ricetti Vineyards are located high in the Eastern hills above Redwood Valley. Each year the red clay soil, ideal exposure and excellent cultural practices bring forth a crop of perfect maturity.

In 1974 the vineyard was picked on October 1 at 25° Brix. After a slow fermentation the wine was racked to small casks and aged until March 1976 when it was bottled. We classify this rich red wine as one of our outstanding Mendocino Zinfandels.

John E. Fetzer

FETZER VINEYARDS

MAYACAMAS

Vintage   1968

Late Harvest
ZINFANDEL

ALCOHOL 17% BY VOLUME
PRODUCED AND BOTTLED BY

Mayacamas Vineyards

NAPA, CALIFORNIA

Clos Du Val

**1972
ZINFANDEL**
Napa Valley

Made and Bottled by
CLOS DU VAL WINE CO LTD
Napa California
Alcohol 13% per Volume

VINTAGE 1973

ALMADÉN

California
ZINFANDEL

A remarkable red wine of intense varietal character
and bouquet that is reminiscent of brambles and wild
blackberries. The grapes were grown in the Almadén
Vineyards of San Benito and Monterey Counties.

PRODUCED AND BOTTLED BY
Almadén Vineyards, Los Gatos, California
Alcohol 12½% by volume

Vineyards Established 1852

ALMADÉN ZINFANDEL

Here, with its marked varietal bouquet and sprightly
flavor — reminiscent, some would say, of brambles,
dewberries, or wild blackberries — is the first ZIN-
FANDEL ever to carry the ALMADÉN varietal label.
It has much of the freshness and easy charm of Beaujolais, and in the long run wines such as this may well
prove the most popular of all the medium-priced California reds.

The Zinfandel wine unquestionably originated in
Europe, although no one knows precisely where; it was
almost surely brought to this country, among some
300,000 cuttings, by Colonel Haraszthy in 1861. It is
widely grown in California today (although apparently
nowhere else in the world). The selected best, given
proper care and aged in small oak barrels, as at Almadén, have remarkable character and class. This is a
typical and a very good one.

The vineyards from which it comes are in the heart
of one of America's great wine districts—the fine wine
vineyards of Northern California. Here the cool nights
and warm days enable the grapes to reach perfection.
Climate, soil and exposure are at their best, remarkably
like those of the famous wine lands of Europe.

PART II
FRENCH WINES

Introduction to French Wines

Thanks to the creation of a French regulatory organization known as the Institut National des Appellations d'Origines des Vins et des Eaux-de-Vie (The National Institute of Appellations of Origin for Wine and Spirits, abbreviated as INAO), the French wine label is, in many ways, much easier to decipher than the California label, even if you are not a French scholar. The Institut, created in 1935 by the French legislature, serves an an advisory board to the minister of agriculture. It establishes all rules and regulations governing the production of French wine, and through its legal arm, La Répression des Fraudes (The Service of the Repression of Fraud), insures that these regulations are being followed at all times.

It was INAO that established the two major categories of French wine: (1) Appellation d'Origine Contrôlée (Controlled Appellation of Origin, abbreviated AOC), and (2) Vins Délimités de Qualité Supérieure (Delimited Wines of Superior Quality, abbreviated VDQS).

The AOC is the higher rating of the two because its rules are somewhat more stringent than those of the VDQS category. Most of the French wines found in the United States, including all of the great châteaux wines of BORDEAUX, have the Appellation Contrôlée expression on their labels. Even though the VDQS rating is second in the hierarchy of French wine, it is a very respectable classification. Certain VDQS wines even equal some AOC wines in quality. The CÔTES DE PROVENCE rosé (soon to become a member of the AOC category) is just one example of a fine VDQS wine. Both the AOC and the VDQS categories have strict controls pertaining to such things as (1) the types of grapes to be planted within a particular region, (2) the number of vines to be grown per acre, (3) the maximum number of gallons of wine that may be produced from each acre of vines, (4) the methods of production, and (5) the minimum alcoholic content of a wine.

The Appellation Contrôlée laws have a twofold purpose. First, they protect the consumer who is looking for a quality product. Second, they help the wine producer by guaranteeing to the public the authenticity of the wine he has made. The word "authentic" is the key to the appellation system, because the AOC and VDQS categories guarantee that when a label states that a wine has come from a specific geographical area, it was in fact produced in that area. The system cannot, however, guarantee the quality of a wine for any given year. It is true that in order to obtain the AOC or VDQS rating, producers within a particular region must follow prescribed procedures, which are designed to enhance the quality of their wine. But unfortunately, no one can guarantee good wine-growing weather, a vital factor in the production of quality wine.

It is sometimes the case that even the very best châteaux of Bordeaux cannot make good wine in a year when weather conditions were not kind to the grape. The very dreary 1965 and 1968 vintages attest to this fact. The National Institute of Appellations of Origin does accomplish its assigned task nonetheless: It protects the *origin* of a wine and establishes strict standards for its production. This in itself significantly improves the chances for the making of quality wine.

One of the essential differences between a California wine label and a French label lies in the naming of the wine. As we have seen, California varietal wines are named according to the grape used to make them. But virtually all French wine names refer to either the region, the district, or the commune where the wine was produced rather than to different types of grapes (although there are some exceptions to the general rule). Under this system, the type of grape or grapes found in the wine is implicit in the place name. For example, the SAUVIGNON BLANC is the only grape allowed in a wine calling itself SANCERRE (a wine district of the Loire Valley). In addition to providing information about the grape, the name also tells you that this wine was produced within the district of Sancerre. The words "Appellation Contrôlée" on the label will confirm the wine's place of origin, Sancerre. Briefly, that is how the French system of appellations works.

A major pitfall when buying French wine is to be attracted to a particular bottle because of its dressy or colorful label. Remember, an attractive label has no bearing on the quality of the wine. One must rely solely on the facts that the label provides: the appellation, the name of the négociant or château, and the vintage date. Wine buying is further complicated by the many unfamiliar regional names and expressions that often appear on French wine labels. In the following chapters on the principal wine regions of France, I will attempt to alleviate as much confusion as possible in order to make the search for French wine a little more predictable and pleasant.

Terms Common to French Wine Labels

Clos   Literally means an enclosed area. In some portions of France the word "clos" is used to designate small parcels of land where grapes are grown and wine is made. If a wine is from an officially designated clos it will probably be quite good, but not necessarily better than a wine that does not have the term "clos" on the label.

Cru   A cru (growth) within a district refers to a particular vineyard, usually one that produces a wine of superior quality. In BORDEAUX the most outstanding wines of the region are known as the GRANDS CRUS CLASSÉS (Great Classified Growths). In CHABLIS and in other parts of BURGUNDY, GRAND CRU and PREMIER CRU denote the best wines. In ALSACE as well, the expression "Grand Cru" is reserved for only the finest wines.

Eleveur   The man or company in charge of a wine's aging and development. The word "éleveur" is most often used to refer to a cattle breeder, but its meaning has been extended to include those individuals who raise wine. "Elevé," the past participle of the French verb élever (to raise), will often precede the name of the person responsible for raising the wine. Frequently, the négociant is also the éleveur.

Marque Déposée Registered trademark.

Mis(e) en Bouteilles au Château (Bottled at the château), Mise(e) en Bouteilles au or du Domaine (Estate Bottled), and Mis(e) en Bouteilles à la Propriété (Bottled on the property) These expressions mean that the wine has been bottled at its place of production and has not been shipped to some other area for bottling, as is sometimes the case. The less a wine travels, the better, so a château or proprietary bottling usually indicates a wine of a somewhat higher quality than most. The designation "Mis(e) en bouteilles au château" is seen almost exclusively on wine labels from BORDEAUX. In most of the other wine regions of France where the word "château" is not used to designate a vineyard, the remaining expressions will be found.

There are several expressions similar in phrasing to those listed above, but which have no real significance in terms of quality. They include: Mis(e) en bouteilles dans nos caves or nos chais (Bottled in our cellars); Mis(e) en bouteilles par—, followed by the name of a négociant; Mis(e) en bouteilles dans la région de production (Bottled in the region of production).

Propriétaire-Récoltant (Owner and harvester), and Propriétaire-Viticulteur (Owner and wine grower) These words usually follow the name of the individual responsible for growing the grapes and/or producing the wine.

Servir frais One can find this expression on many white wine and rosé wine labels. It means "Serve chilled." One to one and a half hours in a refrigerator or ice bucket should be sufficient. If a wine is underchilled it will have no flavor; if overchilled it will lose its distinctive characteristics and balance. When a wine bottle becomes too cold, allow it to warm up gradually at room temperature before pouring the wine.

Alsace

The province of Alsace is situated in the Northeast and forms the border between France and Germany. Its location has made it susceptible to frequent attacks, and historically its national loyalties have been divided between France and Germany. Today, Alsace waves the tricolor, but if one strolls down the ancient cobblestoned streets of Strasbourg, its capital, one will notice the German influence in the architectural designs of the buildings and in the dialect spoken by many of its inhabitants. French is, of course, the first language of the region, for the Alsatians have always considered themselves to be French.

Alsace is one of the most beautiful provinces in all of France, and it is certainly the most enchanting, with its picturesque storybook villages nestled in between the green hills of the Vosges mountains and surrounded by vineyards for as far as the eye can see. This region certainly does not lack natural beauty, nor does it lack outstanding cuisine. It seems that the traveler can always find restaurants with at least one Michelin star as he takes the beautiful wine road, "La Route du Vin," from Marlenheim in the north to Thann in the south.

The wines of Alsace have benefited from an Appellation Contrôlée since 1962, making them newcomers to the AOC category. The majority of wine produced here is white and dry, but some rosé and a very small quantity of red wine from the PINOT NOIR grape are also made. The wines of Alsace are easily recognizable because they come in a tall slender bottle known as the *flûte*.

Alsace is an exception to the general rule concerning how French wines are named. Most French wines receive their name from the region, district, commune, or vineyard that produced them. But Alsace wines, like the varietal wines of California, are named according to the grape variety from which they are made. The most important grapes of Alsace are RIESLING, GEWURZ-TRAMINER, SYLVANER, PINOT BLANC, PINOT GRIS (Tokay d'Alsace), and MUSCAT. Of these, the Riesling, Gewurztraminer, and Sylvaner are the wines that will be most frequently seen in wine shops. Excellent examples of these wines are usually available for less than $5.00.

One of the most frequent mistakes made by American wine buyers is to associate the wines of Alsace with those of Germany. It is true that both Alsace and Germany produce white wine, but that is where the similarity ends. Alsace wines are distinctively French and are vinified in the French, not the German, tradition. Alsace wines are dry and can therefore accompany a meal. The vast majority of German wines are sweet dessert wines that do not complement meals. The dry white wines of Alsace are superb accompaniments for all of those dishes that call for white wine.

Alsace Vintages

It is not widely known that the noble white wines of Alsace, especially the RIESLING and the GEWURZTRAMINER, can age very well, if they are from exceptional vintages. It is not unusual for certain wines to last for fifteen years or more if they are from vintages like 1959, a great year in Alsace. The most outstanding vintages of recent times are 1971 and 1976. Generally, however, the white wines from Alsace should be consumed when they are young— that is, within four to five years past the vintage date on the label. Those vintages that are currently showing very well are 1973, 1974, and 1975.

Alsace The appellation Alsace or Vin d'Alsace is used for all of the wines of the region entitled to this Appellation Contrôlée. Certain wines coming from superior vineyards may use the name of that vineyard on the label, like Clos Gaensbroennel, Clos Ste. Hune, Mamburg, Schoenenberg, Kaefferkopf.

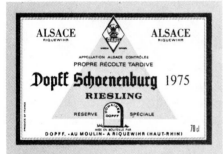

Edelzwicker This is not the name of a grape but of a dry white wine made from a blend of some of the better grape varieties of Alsace.

Gewurztraminer   This name means Spicy Traminer, and that's exactly the way this wine tastes, spicy. In good years, the Gewurztraminer will display its unique qualities by yielding a wine that is flowery, spicy, and perfumed. Gewurztraminer is a dry white wine that ages very well if from an exceptional vintage. It is probably the most distinctive of all the wines from the Alsace region and is, without a doubt, one of the very best.

Muscat   It is extremely rare to find a dry wine made from the Muscat grape, but such a wine exists in Alsace. The Muscat produces a fruity and flowery white wine that makes a fine apéritif, especially for a party. Unfortunately, the Muscat is a rather hard wine to find in the United States.

Pinot Blanc   The Pinot Blanc grape produces a very drinkable dry white wine of good quality.

64

Pinot Gris   This grape is also called Tokay d'Alsace. It yields a very full-bodied dry white wine of excellent quality. A Pinot Gris goes very well with stronger meats, especially game.

Pinot Noir   This grape is used to make the Rosé d'Alsace and a very limited quantity of red wine.

Riesling   The Riesling is considered by many to be the noblest of all Alsace grapes. It gives a very dry white wine that contains the delicate and subtle flavor of flowers and spice. One would be wholly justified in describing the Riesling as a wine of considerable breed and elegance.

Sylvaner   The Sylvaner grape produces a dry, light white wine that makes a fine accompaniment to simple meals. The Sylvaner is a reasonably priced all-purpose white wine that often sells for less than $3.00.

Vendange Tardive (LATE HARVEST)   A late harvest wine is made from grapes that have been allowed to ripen for an extended period of time, beyond the usual harvest date. It is, consequently, richer (and sometimes sweeter) than a wine produced from grapes harvested at the traditional time.

66

Bordeaux

The Bordeaux region of southwestern France is certainly one of the most important and impressive wine-producing areas of that country. Its districts are responsible for many outstanding red and white wines that have been respected throughout the world for more than 120 years. Almost everyone, wine and whiskey lover alike, is familiar with the names of the greatest châteaux of Bordeaux: Haut-Brion, Lafite-Rothschild, Latour, Margaux, and Mouton-Rothschild. According to many wine experts and enthusiasts, they represent the pinnacle of red wine perfection. In good years, and when mature, they are fragrant, smooth, full bodied, and long lived. But Bordeaux did not build its reputation on red wine alone, for some of the best dry and sweet white wines of France come from this region. Château Carbonnieux, Domaine de Chevalier, Château Laville-Haut-Brion, Château d'Yquem, and Château La Tour Blanche (to mention just a few) are names that have become synonymous with quality white wine.

Some of the wines mentioned above are among the most expensive of all French wines, but there are still many affordable bottles of Bordeaux to be found. Before one can find a good wine at a reasonable price, one must first understand how the Bordeaux classification system works.

All red Bordeaux wine is made from a combination of the following grapes: CABERNET SAUVIGNON, Cabernet Franc, MERLOT, MALBEC, and Petit Verdot. The excellent white wines, both dry and sweet, come from the SAUVIGNON BLANC, SEMILLON, and MUSCADELLE grapes. The châteaux all have their traditional blending formulas. Some use more Cabernet Sauvignon for their red wines, others use more Merlot. For white wines the Sauvignon Blanc tends to be the dominant variety. Percentages are not mentioned on the label, as is sometimes done in California, but it is not necessary to do so because the better châteaux have traditionally used a high percentage of the finest grapes.

There are three types of Bordeaux appellations: regional (very general), district (more specific), and communal (very specific). A regional appellation such as Bordeaux or Bordeaux Supérieur is the most general kind. These wines are usually of average quality, but occasionally good values may be found. Wines with a regional appellation usually come from lesser vineyards of Bordeaux.

There are five major wine districts of Bordeaux: MÉDOC, GRAVES, SAUTERNES, SAINT ÉMILION, and POMEROL. Wine labels that carry the name of one of these districts, with no further details concerning the origin of the wine (like the name of a château) indicate that the wine will probably be of good quality. It will, in all likelihood, be much better than a wine with a regional appellation because the grapes were harvested within the district named on the label. This means that the wine should have some of the taste characteristics associated with the better wines of that district.

The communal appellation is the most specific. It means that the wine comes from a delimited area within a district. This area is very small in comparison to the size of a district and the regulations controlling the use of a communal appellation on a label are very restricted. This category really applies only to the Médoc district because it is here that one finds such communal appellations on wine labels as Pauillac, Margaux, Saint Julien, Saint Estèphe, Moulis. A communal appellation is very prestigious as long as it is accompanied by the name of a good château. If no château is mentioned on the label, the wine will probably be quite good, but the better values lie in wines that have both the communal appellation *and* the name of a château.

Note that since Saint Emilion, Pomerol, Graves, and Sauternes do not have communal appellations, the district appellation plus the name of one of the better châteaux is all that is needed on the label to show that the wine is a good one. The vintage year is also an important factor when choosing any wine from Bordeaux because the quality of the wine varies from year to year.

The Château

The very best wines of Bordeaux all come from châteaux. "Château" is another name for a small vineyard where grapes are grown and where wine is produced and bottled. The existence of a physical structure called a château is not necessary in order for a vineyard to use the word on its label, but there must be a self-contained area with all of the necessary elements for wine production. A good wine from Bordeaux will always have the word "château" or "domaine" in its title. The wine buyer would do well, therefore, to be familiar with the names of the better châteaux. By "better" I do not mean most expensive, because many very excellent château wines are reasonably priced. But all wine enthusiasts should be aware of the famous and often very expensive wines of Bordeaux so that they will be able to make price comparisons between these wines and the less expensive wines coming from smaller châteaux. In addition, I would think that anyone who is truly interested either in the study of wine or in browsing through wine shops would want to be able to recognize famous wine names just for his or her own personal edification. Even though I cannot afford to buy them, I have feelings of great satisfaction (and envy) when I see a bottle of Château Latour, Château Margaux, Château Mouton-Rothschild, Château d'Yquem, Château Haut-Brion, or Château Lafite-Rothschild lying quietly on the rack of a wine shop. Knowing that they are available (even if they are not affordable) is very reassuring.

As one can see, Bordeaux is a château-oriented wine region. Even though the names of particular châteaux are not appellations of origin per se, they are protected by French law and do serve as guarantees to the consumer. Most châteaux have long wine-making traditions behind them, and the better ones are always trying to maintain the high standards that their customers have come to expect. No other region practices self-regulation as much as Bordeaux. That is precisely one of the reasons why it is so hard to find wines from any other part of the world that can match those of this region.

I hate to revive old and sordid tales, but many people still wonder about the Bordeaux wine scandal (dubbed "winegate") of 1973. This unfortunate occurrence centers around one of the most famous, and supposedly reputable, Bordeaux shipping firms, Cruse et Fils Frères. The Cruse cousins were convicted in 1974 of conspiring to mislabel some of their wine. Apparently they bought cheap red wine from the lesser vineyards of France (and perhaps Algeria) and tried to label it as wine coming from prestigious Bordeaux districts such as Médoc and Pomerol. The wine had no legal right to an Appellation Contrôlée, but by the time it reached the bottle it had one.

One very important point that must be made is that *no* château was in any way tainted by the scandal. The inferior wine was not being passed off as Lafite, Margaux, or Mouton, and individual châteaux did not participate in the fraudulent scheme. Consequently, only wines with the Cruse label are suspect.

It would be very unfair to generalize about the scandal by saying that since the firm of Cruse attempted to bottle fraudulent wine, all Bordeaux shipping firms and châteaux are guilty of the same crime. If all wine from Bordeaux were fraudulent, the French wine trade would soon be out of business. It is in the interest (financial and otherwise) of every person in the wine business to produce, bottle, and sell a quality product. Consumers are increasing their knowledge of wine every day and are able to spot bad wine. It would be difficult for a major château to get away with selling an inferior wine for an extended period of time. As with any consumer-oriented business, a bad product results in a poor reputation and loss of sales. The vast majority of wine producers in Bordeaux, especially those involved with the classified châteaux, are proud of their illustrious wine-producing heritage and want to see that heritage continue undisturbed.

70

Bordeaux Vintages

The best years for red Bordeaux wine are 1961 (outstanding), 1962, 1964, 1966 (outstanding), 1967, 1969, 1970 (outstanding), 1971, 1973, 1975. The 1967 and 1973 vintages should be drunk now because they will not last much longer. Probably the best buys at the present time are the wines of the very excellent 1970 vintage. Buy these wines now, while they are still reasonably priced, and let them mature in your cellar until 1978 or 1980. Certain wines of the 1970 vintage are drinkable now, but in general they are still a bit tannic (astringent). They should make fine drinking in a few years and will last for some time to come. The very young 1975 vintage shows a great deal of promise and should prove to be another excellent or even outstanding year for red Bordeaux. Buy the 1975s while they are young, but do not drink them for a while. The superb wines of the 1961 vintage are to be sampled whenever they can be found and afforded. The 1966s are more reasonably priced, but like the 1961s, they are rather scarce.

Better white wine vintages include 1970, 1971, 1974, 1975. The 1970 and 1971 vintages were particularly good in the SAUTERNES district, where rich sweet dessert wines are made. These vintages are not too old to buy if the wines come from the finer châteaux. The wines of Sauternes age very well and unlike most other white wines actually improve as they grow older.

GRAVES

The Graves appellation is given to both red and white wines. "Graves Supérieur" is reserved for white wines alone. There are no communal appellations in Graves as there are in the MÉDOC, so the buyer should spend more time looking for the name of a château rather than trying to search for a more specific appellation of origin. The Graves appellation, along with the name of a good château and vintage date, is your assurance of quality.

The red wines of Graves are among the most famous in the world, thanks to the reputation established by CHÂTEAU HAUT-

BRION, the only vineyard of Graves to be classified with the wines of the Médoc in 1855. Today Château Haut-Brion is considered to be the best of the CRUS CLASSÉS of Graves, its illustrious heritage setting it apart from all of the other wines of the district. Haut Brion also produces a very small quantity of excellent white wine that is rather difficult to find. If you do find a bottle you may have second thoughts about buying it, because it is expensive (about $20.00). In good years, the red Haut Brion has an even higher price tag. The 1961 vintage sells for about $63.00 a bottle.

Even though Château Haut-Brion is one of the most expensive wines of France, do not be turned off by the wines of Graves, for there are many excellent examples of both red and white wines of the district that sell for less than $6.00.

An official classification of the best châteaux of the Graves district was established in 1953 and revised in 1959. These châteaux are known as the Crus Classés. Note that both red and white wines are included in the classification.

Château Haut-Brion[1]
Château La Mission Haut-Brion[1]
Château Haut Bailly[1]
Domaine de Chevalier[3]
Château de Fieuzal[1]
Château Carbonnieux[3]
Château Malartic-Lagravière[3]
Château' Latour-Martillac[3]
Château Latour-Haut-Brion[1]
Château Smith-Haut-Lafitte[1]
Château Olivier[3]
Château Bouscaut[3]
Château Pape Clement[1]
Château Couhins[2]
Château Laville-Haut-Brion[2]

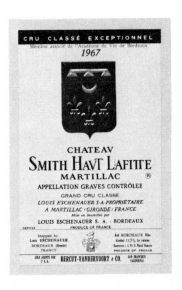

[1] Only the red wines have been classified as Grands Crus.
[2] Only the white wines have been classified as Grands Crus.
[3] Both red and white wines have been classified as Grands Crus.

MÉDOC

The Médoc is the most famous of the Bordeaux wine districts. Its red wines, heralded for many years as the finest produced in France, are superb, but they can be very tannic when young. To fully enjoy these fine wines, one must have the patience to wait until they are mature. If the wine is from a particularly good vintage and château, it is not unusual to wait at least ten years before opening it. Wines from the best châteaux (Lafite-Rothschild, Latour, Margaux, Mouton-Rothschild) sometimes take twenty or thirty years to reach maturity and may last sixty years or more. Generally the lesser classified growths and the CRUS BOURGEOIS are ready to drink in five or ten years' time.

I have found, much to my dismay, that many novices refuse to buy Bordeaux wines (and for that matter Burgundies as well) because they believe that such wines will always taste harsh and tannic. It is true, there is nothing more unpleasant than a young red Bordeaux that is astringent and lacking in fruit. But given the proper amount of time, they can be transformed into very smooth and agreeable wines. Waiting until a red Médoc (or any red Bordeaux) is mature enables you to receive the best value for your money as well as the most wine-drinking pleasure.

Commune
The Médoc is divided into communes that have their own appellations. The very finest wines of Médoc come

from the communes of Margaux, Pauillac, Saint Estèphe, and
Saint Julien. Wines of a somewhat lesser quality come from
the communes of Listrac and Moulis.

Cru Bourgeois This category lists those vineyards of the
Médoc whose wines do not meet the standards of the CRUS
CLASSÉS yet are of a high quality. There are three rankings
within the Cru Bourgeois and each designates a particular
quality of wine: Crus Exceptionnels, Crus Bourgeois Supéri-
eurs, and Crus Bourgeois. Some very fine Crus Bourgeois Su-
périeurs and Crus Bourgeois can be found for less than $5.00 a
bottle, but the Crus Exceptionnels will sell for several dollars
more, depending upon the vintage.

Two further points should be made in connection with this
category. First, the designations Cru Exceptionnel, Cru Bourgeois Supérieur, and Cru Bourgeois are not appellations of
origin. They provide information about the relative quality of
the wine but not about where it was produced. Note that each
wine within the different categories does have a controlled appellation of origin. Some of the finest Crus Bourgeois have
very impressive *communal* appellations like Château Phélan
Ségur (Cru Bourgeois Supérieur), which comes from the commune of Saint Estèphe, and Château Gloria (Cru Bourgeois
Supérieur) from the commune of Saint Julien.

Second, certain châteaux entitled to use the expression "Cru
Exceptionnel," "Cru Bourgeois Supérieur," or "Cru Bourgeois"

on their labels choose not to do so. It becomes important, therefore, to be aware of the names of some of the châteaux that constitute the Cru Bourgeois classification:

CRUS EXCEPTIONNELS

Château Angludet
Château Bel Air-Marquis d'Aligre
Château Chasse-Spleen
Château La Couronne
Château Moulin-Riche
Château Poujeaux-Theil
Château de Villegeorge

CRUS BOURGEOIS SUPÉRIEURS

Château Beau-Site
Château Capbern
Château Citran
Château Dutruch-Grand-Poujeaux
Château Fourcas-Dupre
Château Fourcas-Hosten
Château Gloria
Château Lanessan
Château Meyney
Château de Malleret
Château Paveil-de-Luze
Château Phélan-Ségur
Château Siran

CORDIER

CHÂTEAU
MEYNEY

Prieuré
des Couleys

APPELLATION SAINT-ESTÈPHE CONTROLÉE

1970

MISE EN BOUTEILLES
AU CHÂTEAU

Georges Cordier
Propriétaire

73 d

EXPORTATION STRICTEMENT RESERVÉE

PRODUCE OF FRANCE   IMPRIMÉ EN FRANCE

1962

APPELLATION S.JULIEN CONTROLÉE

Château
Gloria
St. Julien

Henri Martin
PROPRIÉTAIRE A S.JULIEN-BEYCHEVELLE

Mis en bouteilles au Château

1970
Château de Malleret

CRU BOURGEOIS SUPÉRIEUR

APPELLATION HAUT-MÉDOC CONTROLÉE

A. de Luze & Fils

NÉGOCIANTS A BORDEAUX (GIRONDE)

RED BORDEAUX WINE · PRODUCT OF FRANCE · SHIPPED BY
A. de LUZE & FILS NEGOCIANTS A BORDEAUX (GIRONDE)
NET CONTENTS 1 PINT 8.6 FLUID OUNCES · TABLE WINE
IMPORTED BY
SHAW-ROSS IMPORTERS, INC.
MIAMI, FLORIDA

CHÂTEAU LANESSAN

MÉDOC

1973

Delbos-Bouteiller

MIS EN BOUTEILLE AU CHATEAU

APPELLATION HAUT-MÉDOC CONTROLÉE

BOUTEILLER, PROPRIÉTAIRE A CUSSAC (GIRONDE) 73 d

PRODUCE OF FRANCE

CHÂTEAU
PAVEIL de LUZE
HAUT-MÉDOC

APPELLATION HAUT-MÉDOC CONTROLÉE

1970

A. de Luze & Fils

NÉGOCIANTS A BORDEAUX (GIRONDE)

RED BORDEAUX WINE · PRODUCT OF FRANCE · SHIPPED BY
A. de LUZE & FILS NEGOCIANTS A BORDEAUX GIRONDE
NET CONTENTS: 12 FLUID OUNCES · TABLE WINE
Imported by
SHAW-ROSS IMPORTERS, INC.
MIAMI, FLORIDA

Château Barateau
Château Bel Orme
Château Coufran
Château Cap de Haut
Château Duroc-Milon
Château Latour de Haut-Moulin
Château Loudenne
Château Maucaillou
Château McCarthy-Moula
Château Les Ormes-de-Pez
Château de Pez
Château Sénéjac
Château Verdignan

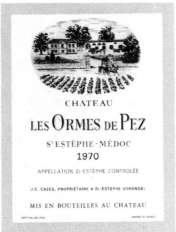

Crus Classés (Classified Growths)   Bordeaux is probably the most organized wine region in France because all of its
better châteaux have been ranked. This practice began in 1855
with the classification of the finest châteaux of the Médoc,
called the Crus Classés. These wines represent the very best of
the district and should be given serious consideration by the
wine enthusiast. Some particularly good values are found on
the Fifth Growth level (Château Belgrave, Château Croizet-
Bages, Château Cantemerle). Though the châteaux were originally ranked according to quality and price, many noted authorities believe that the 1855 classification is in need of an

81

overhaul, since certain châteaux ranked then as Fourth or Fifth Growths deserve a higher rating today, while others on the Second and Third levels have diminished in quality. I suspect that we will be seeing a reevaluation of the 1855 classification in the near future.

Some First and Second Growth wines will use the expression "Premier Grand Cru Classe" or "Deuxième Cru Classé" on their labels. Those wines ranked below the Second Growth level will generally use the expression "Grand Cru Classé" (Great Classified Growth), without a numerical designation.

The following is the basic 1855 Médoc Classification, with a few modern-day revisions:

PREMIERS CRUS (FIRST GROWTHS)	COMMUNE
Château Lafite-Rothschild	Pauillac
Château Margaux	Margaux
Château Latour	Pauillac
Château Haut Brion[1]	Pessac (Graves)
Château Mouton-Rothschild[2]	Pauillac

[1]Château Haut-Brion was the only wine from the Graves district to be classified with the wines of the Médoc in 1855.
[2]Château Mouton-Rothschild was given Premier Cru status in 1973. In 1855 Mouton was officially ranked as a Deuxième Cru.

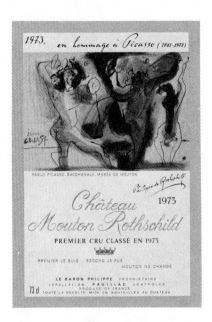

DEUXIÈMES CRUS (SECOND GROWTHS)

COMMUNE

Château Rausan-Segla

Margaux

Château Rauzan-Gassies

Margaux

Château Léoville-Las-Cases

St. Julien

Château Léoville-Poyferre

St. Julien

Château Léoville-Barton	St. Julien
Château Durfort-Vivens	Margaux
Château Gruaud-Larose	St. Julien
Château Lascombes	Margaux
Château Brane-Cantenac	Cantenac-Margaux
Château Pichon-Longueville (Baron)	Pauillac
Château Pichon-Longueville-Lalande	Pauillac
Château Ducru-Beaucaillou	St. Julien
Château Cos d'Estournel	St. Estèphe
Château Montrose	St. Estèphe

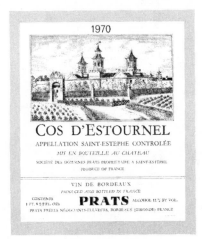

TROISIÈMES CRUS (THIRD GROWTHS)	COMMUNE
Château Kirwan	Cantenac-Margaux
Château d'Issan	Cantenac-Margaux
Château Lagrange	St. Julien
Château Langoa	St. Julien
Château Giscours	Labarde-Margaux
Château Malescot-St. Exupéry	Margaux
Château Cantenac-Brown	Cantenac-Margaux
Château Boyd-Cantenac	Margaux
Château Palmer	Cantenac-Margaux
Château La Lagune	Ludon

Château Desmirail	Margaux
Château Calon-Ségur	St. Estèphe
Château Ferrière	Margaux
Château Marquis d'Alesme Becker	Margaux

QUATRIÈMES CRUS (FOURTH GROWTHS)   COMMUNE

Château St. Pierre	St. Julien
Château Talbot	St. Julien
Château Branaire-Ducru	St. Julien
Château Duhart-Milon-Rothschild	Pauillac
Château Pouget	Cantenac-Margaux
Château La Tour-Carnet	St. Laurent
Château Lafon-Rochet	St. Estèphe
Château Beychevelle	St. Julien
Château Le Prieuré (Prieuré Lichine)	Cantenac-Margaux
Château Marquis de Terme	Margaux

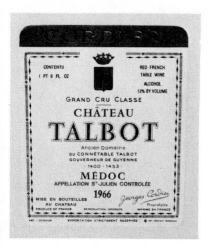

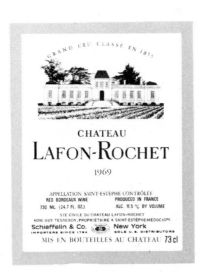

CINQUIÈMES CRUS (FIFTH GROWTHS)	COMMUNE
Château Pontet-Canet	Pauillac
Château Batailley	Pauillac
Château Haut-Batailley	Pauillac
Château Grand-Puy-Lacoste	Pauillac
Château Grand-Puy-Ducasse	Pauillac
Château Lynch-Bages	Pauillac
Château Lynch-Moussas	Pauillac
Château Dauzac	Labarde

88

Château Mouton d'Armailhacq (Mouton Baron Philippe)	Pauillac
Château du Tertre	Arsac
Château Haut-Bages-Libéral	Pauillac
Château Pédesclaux	Pauillac
Château Belgrave	St. Laurent
Château Camensac	St. Laurent
Château Cos Labory	St. Estèphe
Château Clerc-Milon	Pauillac
Château Croizet-Bages	Pauillac
Château Cantemerle	Macau

POMEROL

The red wines of Pomerol are seductively soft and mature more quickly than the wines of the MÉDOC. The individual who wishes to drink a mature and elegant full-bodied wine should pay particular attention to the many fine wines of the Pomerol district.

The most important wines of this area all have the Pomerol appellation, plus the name of a good château. The better châteaux

wines of the district are not inexpensive; they range from about $7.00 up to about $50.00 or more for Château Petrus, the father of all Pomerols. Wines that do not carry the name of a château are often good values, but they are sometimes just as expensive as the best château bottled wines. When possible, purchase those wines coming from the fine châteaux of the district. Note that only red wines are produced in Pomerol.

Château Petrus is considered to be the finest wine of Pomerol. Other excellent wines include:

Château Beauregard
Château Bourgneuf
Château Certan-de-May
Château Certan-Giraud
Château Clinet
Château Clos-du-Clocher
Château Domaine de L'Eglise
Château L'Eglise
Château L'Enclos

91

Château L'Evangile
Château Feytit-Clinet
Château Gazin
Château Gombaude-Guillot
Château Grate-Cap
Château Guillot
Château La Cabane
Château Le Caillou
Château La Commanderie
Château La Conseillante
Château La Croix

Château La Croix-de-Gay
Château La Croix-Saint-Georges
Château La Fleur
Château La Fleur-Pétrus
Château Lagrange
Château La Grave-Trigant-de-Boisset
Château La Pointe
Château Latour-Pomerol
Château La Violette
Château Le Gay
Château Mazeyres
Château Clos Mazeyres
Château Moulinet
Château Nénin
Château Petit-Village
Château Plince
Château Clos Rene
Château Rouget
Château de Sales
Château Taillefer
Château Trotanoy
Vieux Château Certan
Château Vraie-Croix-de-Gay

Lalande-de-Pomerol

Wines with this appellation come from an area located to the north of Pomerol and not from Pomerol itself. They should be considerably less expensive than wines with the Pomerol appellation and are often excellent values.

SAINT ÉMILION

In addition to being the most beautiful of all wine districts, Saint Emilion is known for its production of vigorous, full-bodied red wines of excellent quality. Like the MÉDOCS, these wines are good for laying down in a wine cellar so that they may reach their proper maturity.

The Saint Emilion classification of 1955 contains three categories, each designating a certain level of quality. In descending

order they are (1) Premier Grand Cru Classé, (2) Grand Cru Classé, and (3) Grand Cru.

For purposes of simplification only those châteaux of the first two categories are presented. Actually, there are enough very good wines on the Premier Grand Cru Classé and Grand Cru Classé levels to provide the serious wine enthusiast with a great deal of wine-drinking pleasure. Choose from this list whenever you wish to sample the fine wines of Saint Emilion.

PREMIERS GRANDS CRUS CLASSÉS (FIRST GREAT CLASSIFIED GROWTHS)

A

Château Ausone
Château Cheval Blanc

B
Château Beauséjour
Château Belair
Château Canon
Clos Fourtet
Château Figeac
Château La Gaffelière
Château Magdelaine
Château Pavie
Château Trottevieille

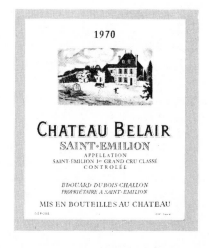

GRANDS CRUS CLASSÉS (GREAT CLASSIFIED GROWTHS)

Château L'Angelus
Château L'Arrosée
Château Balestard-la-Tonnelle
Château Bellevue
Château Bergat
Château Cadet-Bon
Château Cadet-Piola
Château Canon-la-Gaffelière
Château Cap-de-Mourlin
Château La Carte
Château Chapelle-Madeleine

Château Le Chatelet
Château Chauvin
Clos des Jacobins
Clos la Madeleine
Clos Saint Martin
Château La Clotte
Château La Cluzière
Château Corbin
Château Corbin-Michotte
Château La Couspaude
Château Coutet
Château Le Couvent
Château Croque-Michotte
Château Curé-Bon
Château La Dominique
Château Fonplegade
Château Fonroque
Château Franc-Mayne
Château Grand-Barrail-Lamarzelle-Figeac
Château Grand-Corbin Despagne
Château Grand-Corbin-Pecresse
Château Grand-Mayne
Château Grand-Pontet
Château Grandes Murailles
Château Gaudet Saint-Julien
Château Haut-Corbin
Château Haut-Sarpe
Château Jean Faure

Château Larcis Ducasse
Château Lamarzelle
Château Larmande
Château Laroze
Château Lasserre
Château Matras
Château Mauvezin
Château Moulin du Cadet
Château Pavie-Decesse
Château Pavie-Macquin

Château Croque Michotte
Grand Cru Classé
ST EMILION
Geoffrion, Propriétaire
1964

APPELLATION D'ORIGINE CONTRÔLÉE — Mise en bouteille au Château

PRODUCE OF FRANCE

GRAND CRU CLASSÉ

CHATEAU FONPLÉGADE
SAINT-EMILION
APPELLATION SI-EMILION GRAND CRU CLASSÉ CONTRÔLÉE
◄ 1970 ►
VIGNOBLES MOUEIX PÈRE & FILS
PROPRIÉTAIRE A SAINT-EMILION (GIRONDE)
MIS EN BOUTEILLES AU CHATEAU

1970

CHÂTEAU
Franc-Mayne
GRAND CRU CLASSÉ
SAINT-ÉMILION
Appellation Saint-Émilion Grand Cru Classé Contrôlée
J. THEILLASSOUBRE, Propriétaire à Saint-Émilion
MIS EN BOUTEILLES AU CHATEAU
PRODUCE OF FRANCE
BERCUT-VANDERVOORT & Co.
SOLE U.S. AGENTS   SAN FRANCISCO · CALIF.
RED BORDEAUX WINE   ALCOHOL 12% BY VOL.   CONTENTS: 1 PT 8 FL. OZS

MIS EN BOUTEILLES AU CHATEAU

Château Grand Barrail
Lamarzelle Figeac
GRAND CRU CLASSÉ
Saint-Emilion
APPELLATION SI-EMILION GRAND CRU CLASSÉ CONTRÔLÉE
1969
EDMOND CARRÈRE
PROPRIÉTAIRE A SAINT-EMILION-GIRONDE

AUTHENTICITÉ ET QUALITÉ GARANTIES
PAR LA
MISE EN BOUTEILLE AU CHATEAU

1959

Château
La Tour Figeac
SAINT ÉMILION
Appellation
Saint-Émilion Grand Cru Classé
Contrôlée

SOCIÉTÉ CIVILE DU CHATEAU LATOUR FIGEAC
PROPRIÉTAIRE A SAINT-ÉMILION-GIRONDE
Louis Rapin, Gérant

Château Ripeau
ST-ÉMILION
GRAND CRU CLASSÉ

APPELLATION SAINT-ÉMILION CONTRÔLÉE
1972   73 cl

SIÈGE SOCIAL   ALEXIS   SUCCURSALES
BORDEAUX   LICHINE & Cº
(Gironde)
PRODUCE OF FRANCE

Château Pavillon-Cadet
Château Petit-Faurie-de-Souchard
Château Petit-Faurie-de-Soutard
Château Le Prieuré
Château Ripeau
Château Saint-Georges-Cote-Pavie
Château Sansonnet
Château Soutard
Château Tertre-Daugay
Château La Tour-du-Pin-Figeac
Château La Tour-Figeac
Château Trimoulet
Château Trois Moulins
Château Troplong-Mondot
Château Villemaurine
Château Yon-Figeac

Some very fine wines of Grand Cru status are Château La Grâce Dieu, Château Lapelletrie, and Château Monbousquet.

The Saint Emilion label can be used to identify a wine's rank within the official classification, because it will often contain one of the following appellations: Saint Emilion Ier Grand Cru Classé, Saint Emilion Grand Cru Classé, or Saint Emilion Grand Cru.

Though the label from Château Ausone does not carry the Saint Emilion Ier Grand Cru Classé designation, one can rest assured that the wine belongs to this category. Château Ausone, along with Château Cheval Blanc, is considered to be Saint Emilion's best wine. These are the two most expensive wines of the district.

Puisseguin Saint-Emilion   Though the COMMUNE of Puisseguin may attach the district name of Saint-Emilion to its own, one should not think that its wines are of a quality equal to those that carry only the name Saint Emilion. The best wines of the district have the Saint Emilion appellation without the name of a commune before it. A wine with the Puisseguin-Saint-Emilion appellation is not of the same stature as the classified wines previously mentioned. Look for some of the less expensive classified growths of Saint-Emilion before choosing this wine.

SAUTERNES

The Sauternes district lies south of GRAVES, and comprises five important COMMUNES: Sauternes, BARSAC, Bommes, Preignac, and Fargues. The great sweet white wines made here are born as a result of a rather distinctive procedure of growing and harvesting grapes. In most other districts, vine growers are satisfied when their grapes have become ripe. When this occurs they begin to pick. But in Sauternes, ripe is not good enough. If the grapes are not overly ripe (rotten), then the very rich honeylike wine known as Sauternes cannot be made. Contrary to what some people may think, no sugar is added to this wine. Its sweetness is derived naturally by allowing the grapes to remain on the vine until they have been attacked by a mold (*Botrytis Cinerea*), known in France as La Pourriture Noble (Noble Rot). This mold results in a high sugar

content in the grapes, thereby producing a sweet wine. Since the grapes are not all attacked by *Botrytis Cinerea* at the same time, picking is staggered. Only the grapes that have been struck by the Noble Rot are taken; the others are left on the vine until they too have reached the proper state of overripeness. This method of selective picking is called *trie*.

If conditions are not right for the appearance of the mold, a drier wine will be made. But a dry wine from the district is a bad example of a Sauternes, because a good Sauternes is always very rich and very sweet. There are some interesting dry white wines made here (Y, produced at Château d'Yquem), but they are not allowed to use the name "Sauternes" on the label.

All wines from Sauternes are made from a combination of white wine grapes that include SAUVIGNON BLANC, SEMILLON, and MUSCADELLE. Fortunately, the rich wines produced from these grapes are not richly priced. Some of the Premier Cru (First Growth) wines of the district are relatively inexpensive, considering their high quality. For the sweet white wine lover, and for his or her wallet, Sauternes is an oasis amid steep Bordeaux wine prices. Take advantage of the situation while it lasts. Château d'Yquem, the best wine of Sauternes, is an exception; it is always very expensive.

Barsac   Wines from this commune may use either the Sauternes or Barsac appellation on their labels. Some excellent sweet white wines come from Barsac, including Château Climens and Château Coutet, two fine First Growths (Premiers Crus).

The Classification of 1855   The wines of Sauternes were classified in 1855 at the same time as the wines of the MEDOC. The châteaux (with their communes) are ranked in the following order.

PREMIER GRAND CRU (FIRST GREAT GROWTH)   COMMUNE

Château d'Yquem   Sauternes

PREMIERS CRUS (FIRST GROWTHS)	COMMUNE
Château La Tour-Blanche	Bommes
Château Lafaurie-Peyraguey	Bommes
Château Clos Haut-Peyraguey	Bommes
Château Rayne-Vigneau	Bommes
Château Suduiraut	Preignac
Château Coutet	Barsac
Château Climens	Barsac
Château Guiraud	Sauternes
Château Rieussec	Fargues
Château Sigalas-Rabaud	Bommes
Château Rabaud-Promis	Bommes

DEUXIÈMES CRUS (SECOND GROWTHS)	COMMUNE
Château Myrat	Barsac
Château Doisy-Dubroca	Barsac
Château Doisy-Daëne	Barsac
Château Doisy-Védrines	Barsac
Château Filhot	Sauternes
Château d'Arche	Sauternes
Château Broustet	Sauternes
Château Caillou	Barsac
Château Suau	Barsac
Château de Malle	Preignac
Château Romer	Fargues
Château Lamothe	Sauternes
Château Nairac	Barsac

Burgundy

The vineyards of Burgundy produce some of the most elegant red and white wines of France. For many years wine lovers the world over have been drawn, as if by some mysterious force, to the three great wines of the region, ROMANÉE-CONTI, CHAMERTIN, and MONT-RACHET, as well as to many of the "smaller" wines of the area.

Most Americans are familiar with the name "Burgundy" (if not the wine) because there is an extremely large quantity of wine produced in California under that name. But genuine Burgundy, from the province of Bourgogne, cannot be duplicated and is infinitely superior to California's poor imitations.

Good Burgundy is not inexpensive, and unfortunately much of it is overpriced. But some very fine bottles of red and white wine are available at fairly reasonable prices. The key to finding the best wine value lies in the understanding of Burgundy's controlled appellations of origin.

The Burgundy wine region is divided into the following districts:

Chablis
Côte de Nuits ⎤
Côte de Beaune ⎦ Côte d'Or
Chalonnais
Mâconnais
Beaujolais

The four types of controlled appellations within Burgundy correspond to these and other geographical subdivisions. Keep in mind that, as a general rule, "the more specific the appellation, the better the wine." From the very general to the very specific, the appellations are as follows: (1) regional appellations, (2) district appellations, (3) communal or village appellations, and (4) *climats* appellations.

The regional appellation is the most general type of appellation to be seen on a wine label. Bourgogne, Bourgogne Aligoté, and Bourgogne Passetoutgrain are examples of the regional appellation. When one sees an appellation of this kind, it means that the grapes used to make the wine were probably taken from a number of vineyards within the vast Burgundy wine region and blended together. There are some good values in this category, but not too many.

CÔTE DE NUITS, CÔTE DE BEAUNE, MÂCON, and BEAUJOLAIS are examples of the district appellation. Since this appellation is more specific—that is, more limited in area—wines in this category are usually of a higher quality and represent a better value than the wines of the first group. A district appellation such as Côte de

Nuits tells the shopper that the wine was produced from grapes harvested within the territory known as the Côte de Nuits. This district has been defined in terms of area and occupies a relatively small portion of land within Burgundy. If the word "villages" appears on the label, as in "Côte de Nuits-Villages," this means that the area from which the grapes were harvested was even smaller, thereby increasing the likelihood that the wine will be superior to a plain Côte de Nuits.

Now we are approaching true quality, for the communal appellation is even more restricted in terms of area and methods of production than is the district appellation. Some of Burgundy's best wine values are to be found in this category. A COMMUNE or village is a small area within a district that is entitled to lend its name to the wine it produces. NUITS-SAINT-GEORGES, GEVREY-CHAMBERTIN, VOSNE-ROMANÉE, and ALOXE-CORTON are all examples of outstanding communal appellations. The first three communes are part of the Côte de Nuits district, while Aloxe-Corton belongs to the Côte de Beaune district. A wine label with the name "Nuits-Saint-Georges" indicates that the grapes used in the wine were grown

109

within the commune of Nuits-Saint-Georges. Wines with communal appellations are very desirable because they tend to display much more originality and distinction than wines of the two previous categories.

The very finest of all Burgundies come from small vineyards called *climats*. These vineyards produce outstanding wine because of their superior soil, climate, and exposure and their limited number of vines. The *climats* have been grouped into two classifications: Grand Cru (Great Growth) and Premier Cru (First Growth). Grand Cru vineyards may use their own name as appellations for the wines they produce such as Romanée-Conti, La Tâche, Richebourg, Corton, and Chambertin. The wines of this category are ranked higher than wines coming from Premier Cru vineyards and are considered to be the best of the Burgundies. Premier Cru *climats* may use their name on a label along with the expression "Premier Cru" (or "Ier Cru") and the name of the commune where the *climat* (vineyard) is found. It is also possible to

110

see the name of the commune and the vineyard name without the expression "Ier Cru" (or "Premier Cru"). The absence of the term "Premier Cru" does not detract from these wines because they are of Premier Cru status as long as the name of the First Growth vineyard is listed on the label. Use of either Premier Cru or Ier Cru is optional in this case. A third possibility is the name of the commune and either Ier Cru or Premier Cru without the name of the vineyard.

It is advisable to choose a wine that has the name of the vineyard on the label. This way you can be certain of the wine's origin and authenticity. A wine label with the Premier Cru (Ier Cru) expression and no vineyard name indicates that the wine comes from one or more of the First Growth vineyards of the commune.

It should be noted that while a Grand Cru vineyard has a higher standing than a Premier Cru vineyard, a Premier Cru wine is often the better value. Grand Cru Burgundies are generally the most expensive wines of the region.

Burgundy Vintages

The best years for red Burgundies are 1969 (excellent), 1970, 1971 (excellent), 1972, 1973, and 1976 (excellent). White wines from the 1973, 1974, 1975, and 1976 vintages are very good.

In general one should not be too eager to drink a bottle of red Burgundy. Wines with communal appellations from the CÔTE DE NUITS and CÔTE DE BEAUNE should not be opened before they are at least four or five years old. Wines that are from specific vineyards (*climats*) may need several more years before they are ready to drink. If young red Burgundies are allowed to age, they will lose their tannic harshness and become smooth, drinkable wines.

CHABLIS

This very famous district of Burgundy produces only dry white wines made from the CHARDONNAY grape. Vineyard owners have a very difficult time tending the delicate Chardonnay because Chablis is the northernmost of Burgundy's vineyards and is, therefore, susceptible to severe frost. When the weather obliges, the Chardonnay yields a very dry wine of distinction, with a flavor that is said to be "flinty" or "steely." These characteristics make the crisp Chablis a perfect accompaniment to fish, especially shellfish.

Some Chablis wines are produced and bottled at the estate by vineyard owners and will carry the expression "MIS(E) EN BOUTEILLES AU DOMAINE" or "MIS(E) EN BOUTEILLES DU DOMAINE" on the label. Other Chablis are bottled by local shippers (négociants). The wine

112

shopper should be aware of some of the better proprietors and shippers of the Chablis district:

William Fèvre	J. Moreau et Fils
Albert Long-Depaquit	Albert Pic et Fils
Louis Michel	A. Regnard et Fils

There are four controlled appellations of origin in the Chablis district, each of which designates a particular quality of wine. In descending order they are (1) Chablis Grand Cru (2) Chablis Premier Cru (3) Chablis (4) Petit Chablis.

The expression "Chablis Grand Cru" (Great Growth) is the most prestigious of Chablis appellations and may be followed by the name of one of these vineyards:

Blanchots	Les Preuses
Bougros	Valmur
Les Clos	Vaudésir
Grenouilles	

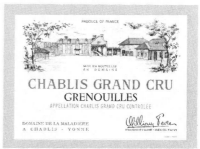

A Grand Cru is the most expensive Chablis, selling at about $8.00 a bottle. In good years, this is a very excellent dry white wine.

There are more than two dozen vineyards entitled to produce the Chablis Premier Cru (First Growth), as opposed to seven for the Grand Cru. Even though standards are somewhat lower for the Premier Cru than they are for the Grand Cru, the Chablis Premier Cru is a wine of high quality that possesses all of the typical characteristics of a fine Chablis. The following vineyards produce the Chablis Premier Cru:

Beauroy	Côte des Prés-Girots
Beugnons	Les Epinottes
Butteaux	Fôrets
Chapelot	Fourchaume
Châtains	Les Fourneaux
Côte de Fontenay	L'Homme-Mort
Côte de Lechet	Les Lys

Mélinots	Troesme
Montée-de-Tonnerre	Vaillon
Montmains	Vaucoupin
Monts-de-Milieu	Vaugiraut
Morein	Vaulorent
Pied-d'Aloup	Vaupulent
Roncières	Vosgros
Séché	

Ranked third in the hierarchy of Chablis wines is the simple Chablis. Generally, a wine with only a Chablis appellation is good, but not as distinguished as one that is of Grand Cru or Premier Cru status.

The least impressive appellation is that of Petit Chablis (Little Chablis). This is a drinkable wine, but it is not one of the better examples of a Chablis.

Chablis Vintages

The best of the recent vintages in Chablis includes 1973, 1974, 1975, and 1976. A Chablis is best when consumed between the time it is bottled until it has reached the age of four or five. In good years, certain Chablis Grands Crus and Premiers Crus can last considerably longer.

116

CÔTE DE NUITS

The best red wines of Burgundy come from this celebrated district that comprises the northern half of the Côte d'Or (Golden Slope). The communes of CHAMBOLLE-MUSIGNY, FIXIN, FLAGEY-ECHÉZEAUX, GEVREY-CHAMBERTIN, MOREY-SAINT-DENIS, NUITS-SAINT-GEORGES, VOSNE-ROMANÉE, and VOUGEOT are all located within the Côte de Nuits, and their wines are considered to be some of the most elegant and distinguished of all French wines. They are full-bodied, rich, and complex and can be conserved for long periods of time in better years. These excellent wines, made from the PINOT NOIR grape, are said to be more "masculine" or aggressive than the wines of Bordeaux. However you characterize the wines from the Côte de Nuits, there is no doubt that they will provide an exciting wine-tasting experience for anyone fortunate enough to partake of them.

Chambolle-Musigny   If a wine label carries this communal appellation without the name of a specific vineyard, the wine will probably be a good one, but not as good as one that comes from a classified *climat* like Musigny, Bonnes Mares, Les Amoureuses, Les Baudes, Aux Beaux Bruns, Les Borniques, Les Charmes, Les Chatelots, Aux Combottes, Les Combottes, Les Cras, Derrière-la-Grange, Les Fousselottes, Les Fuées, Les Groseilles, Les Gruenchers, Les Hauts Doix, Les Lavrottes, Les Noirots, Les Plantes, or Les Sentiers.

Musigny and Bonnes Mares are ranked above the other vineyards (they are Grands Crus—Great Growths) and are entitled to their own appellations. The remaining vineyards, ranked as Premiers Crus (First Growths) may use their names on a label along with the communal name of Chambolle-Musigny. Wines that come from one or more of these vineyards may use the expression "Premier Cru" on the label.

The wines of this COMMUNE are considered to be softer and more delicate than most of the other red wines of the Côte de Nuits. Chambolle-Musigny is known for its fine red wine, but a very small amount of white wine is also produced in the commune, such as the Musigny Blanc.

La Confrérie des Chevaliers du Tastevin (The Brotherhood of the Knights of the Wine-Taster's Cup) This is one of the most prestigious wine organizations in France. It was established in the early 1930s at a time

when the French wine trade was in some financial difficulty. The Chevaliers' mission was to disseminate information to the public on Burgundy and her wines in order to revive the then ailing region. Today, Burgundy thrives, thanks in part to the admirable work of the Confrérie.

The Brotherhood makes its home in the beautiful Château de Vougeot, built by Cistercian monks in the twelfth century. The château sits in the center of the CLOS DE VOUGEOT vineyard watching over the precious red and white wine grapes that have made this area so famous. The château and its surroundings are serene most of the time, but when the Chevaliers from around the world congregate for one of their special dinners (called *chapîtres*), the Vougeot countryside comes alive with gaiety and goodwill inspired by a love for the glorious wines of Burgundy.

In addition to its role as a kind of public relations firm for Burgundian wine, the Confrérie has a panel of wine tasters who seek out particularly noteworthy examples of wines from all of the important COMMUNES of the region. If selected, a wine is given the special label that says "Tastevinage." This means that the wine has been tasted and approved by the Brotherhood's panel of experts. Such a label immediately places the wine above its peers, both in prestige and in price.

The colorful and rather ornate label given by the Brotherhood does not constitute an official controlled appellation. The wine must meet the necessary governmental requirements like any other before it can receive the Appellation

119

d'Origine Contrôlée. The acceptance of a wine by the Confrérie comes after the wine has received its controlled appellation from the National Institute of Appellations of Origin. Being selected by the Brotherhood's wine-tasting panel is simply icing on the cake.

Fixin   This often overlooked COMMUNE of the Côte de Nuits produces some very good and reasonably priced red wine. Since the Fixin area is small and not as well known as the other communes of the Côte, one may be able to find some interesting bargains. The finest vineyards of Fixin are Les Arvelets, Clos du Chapitre, Les Hervelets, Les Meix bas, Clos Napoléon, Clos de la Perrière. These vineyards are classified as Premiers Crus.

Flagey-Echézeaux   The vineyards of this COMMUNE are classified with those of VOSNE-ROMANÉE.

Gevrey-Chambertin   This is one of the most famous COMMUNES of the Côte de Nuits, for the Chambertins have long been considered as some of Burgundy's finest red wines. These are solid, full-bodied wines that often need time in the bottle to soften. A wine with the general Gevrey-Chambertin appellation is often excellent but somewhat expensive at $7.00 to $9.00 a bottle. The alert shopper can sometimes find a wine from one of the classified vineyards (*climats*) of Gevrey-Chambertin for less than he or she would pay for a bottle with a simple Gevrey-Chambertin appellation. The following vine-

CHAMBERTIN
APPELLATION CONTROLÉE
1969 • 1969

DOMAINE JACQUES PRIEUR
Propriétaire à Meursault (Côte-d'Or)
MISE EN BOUTEILLES DU DOMAINE
PRODUCE OF FRANCE

VINTAGE 1971

BOUCHARD PÈRE & FILS
GEVREY-CHAMBERTIN
APPELLATION GEVREY-CHAMBERTIN CONTROLÉE

MIS EN BOUTEILLE PAR LA MAISON
BOUCHARD PÈRE & FILS, NÉGOCIANTS AU CHATEAU, BEAUNE (COTE-D'OR)
PRODUCE OF FRANCE   RED BURGUNDY WINE
ALCOHOL 13% BY VOLUME   CONTENTS 17 FL. OZ.
PRODUCED AND BOTTLED BY : BOUCHARD PÈRE & FILS, BEAUNE
Imported by : HEUBLEIN, INC. HARTFORD, CONNECTICUT

MISE DU DOMAINE   1971
TRADE MARK

CHAMBERTIN
APPELLATION CONTROLÉE

DOMAINE PHILIPPE REMY
GEVREY-CHAMBERTIN (COTE-D'OR) FRANCE

MIS EN BOUTEILLES A LA PROPRIÉTÉ
Médaille d'Or   Paris 1962

CHAMBERTIN
CLOS DE BÈZE
APPELLATION CONTROLÉE

PIERRE GELIN
PROPRIÉTAIRE A FIXIN ET GEVREY-CHAMBERTIN (COTE-D'OR)

Mise en Bouteilles au Domaine
PRODUCE OF FRANCE

CHAPELLE-CHAMBERTIN
Appellation Contrôlée

Domaine CLAIR-DAÜ
Propriétaire à Marsannay-la-Côte (Côte-d'Or)

Joseph Drouhin
RÉCOLTE DU DOMAINE

GRIOTTE-CHAMBERTIN
APPELLATION CONTROLÉE

MIS EN BOUTEILLE PAR
JOSEPH DROUHIN
Maison fondée en 1880
NÉGOCIANT A BEAUNE, COTE-D'OR
AUX CELLIERS DES ROIS DE FRANCE ET DES DUCS DE BOURGOGNE

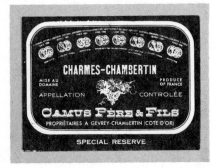

CHARMES-CHAMBERTIN
MISE AU   PRODUCE
DOMAINE   OF FRANCE
APPELLATION   CONTROLÉE

CAMUS PÈRE & FILS
PROPRIÉTAIRES A GEVREY-CHAMBERTIN (COTE D'OR)

SPECIAL RESERVE

121

yards represent the most outstanding *climats* of Gevrey-Chambertin, known as the Grands Crus: Chambertin, Chambertin-Clos-de-Bèze, Chapelle-Chambertin, Charmes-Chambertin, Griotte-Chambertin, Latricières-Chambertin, Mazis-Chambertin, Mazoyères-Chambertin, Ruchottes-Chambertin.

First Growth (Premier Cru) vineyards include Bel Air, Cazetiers, Champeaux, Champonnets, Champitonnois (Petite Chapelle), Cherbaudes, Au Closeau, Clos du Chapitre, Clos Prieur, Clos Saint Jacques (Village Saint Jacques), Combe-aux-Moines, Aux Combottes, Les Corbeaux, Craipillot, Ergots, Estournelles, Le Fonteny, les Gemeaux, Les Goulots, Issarts, Lavaut, La Perrière, Poissenot, Les Varoilles.

Morey-Saint-Denis There is some white wine produced here, but this COMMUNE, like the others of the Côte de Nuits, is renowned for its excellent full-bodied red wine. The Grand Cru vineyards of Morey-Saint-Denis are Bonnes Mares, Clos de la Roche, Clos Saint Denis, Clos de Tart. These superior *climats* are entitled to separate appellations, which will be seen on wine labels without the commune name of Morey-Saint-Denis. Ranked just below them are the following Premier Cru vineyards: Les Bouchots, Calouères, Chabiots, Les Chaffots, Aux Charmes, Les Charrières, Les Chénevery Le Clos Baulet, Clos Bussière, Clos des Lambrays, Le Clos des Ormes, Le Clos Sorbés, Côte Rôtie, Les Faconnières, Les Frémières, Les Froichots, Les Genevrières, Les Gruenchers, Maison Brûlée, Les Mauchamps, Meix-Rentiers, Les Millandes, Monts Luisants, La Riotte, Les Ruchots, Les Sorbés.

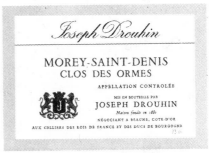

Nuits-Saint-Georges   This is the southernmost of the major wine-producing COMMUNES of the Côte de Nuits. The red wines of Nuits-Saint-Georges are full-flavored and less aggressive than some of the wines from the northern communes. There are only Premier Cru vineyards in Nuits-Saint-Georges; none has been classified as Grand Cru. They are Aux Argillats, Les Argillats, Aux Boudots, Aux Bousselots, Les Cailles, Les Chaboeufs, Aux Chaignots, Chaine Carteau, Aux Champs Per-

123

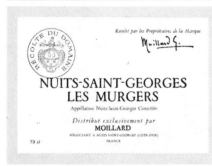

124

drix, Clos des Argillières, Clos Arlots, Clos des Corvées, Clos des Forêts, Clos de la Maréchale, Clos Saint Marc, Les Corvées-Paget, Aux Cras, Aux Crots, Aux Damodes, Les Didiers, Les Haut Pruliers, Aux Murgers, Aux Perdrix, La Perrière, Perrière-Noblet, Les Porets, Les Poulettes, Les Procès, Les Pruliers, La Richmone, La Roncière, Rue de Chaux, Les Saint-Georges, Aux Thorey, Les Vallerots, Les Vaucrains, Aux Vignes Rondes.

If one desires a truly characteristic Nuits-Saint-Georges, he or she will choose a wine with a vineyard name on the label and not just the commune name "Nuits-Saint-Georges."

Vosne-Romanée For hundreds of years the French have looked to this COMMUNE when in search of wine excellence, and Vosne-Romanée has usually fulfilled their high expectations by producing such outstanding Grand Cru wines as

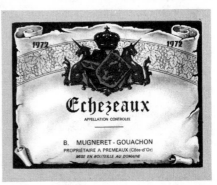

Echézeaux, Grands Echézeaux, Richebourg, La Romanée, Romanée-Conti, Romanée-Saint-Vivant, and La Tâche. They represent the very finest wines of the commune and are entitled to their own appellations. These wines are usually quite expensive ($20.00 and up).

The First Growth (Premier Cru) vineyards of Vosne-Romanée are known for their fine wines of high quality, which do not, however, attain the same level of distinction as the Grands Crus. Wine labels may include the names of the following First Growth vineyards, provided that they follow the communal name "Vosne-Romanée": Les Beaux Monts, Aux Brûlées, Les Chaumes, Le Clos des Réas, Les Gaudichots, La Grande Rue, Aux Malconsorts, Les Petits Monts, Les Reignots, Les Suchots.

Vougeot   The glorious medieval château of Vougeot, home of Burgundy's prestigious wine society, LA CONFRÉRIE DES CHEVAL- IERS DU TASTEVIN, guards the famed Clos de Vougeot vineyard, the only Grand Cru vineyard of the COMMUNE. The red wine from the Clos de Vougeot is very good but expensive, starting at about $10.00 and going higher for better vintages. There is also a very fragrant and flavorful white wine produced here, called Clos Blanc de Vougeot, from the vineyard of L'Héritier Guyot. The white wine is priced at about $12.00, but, like those of the red, prices vary according to the vintage. The Pre- mier Cru (First Growth) vineyards of Vougeot are Clos Blanc

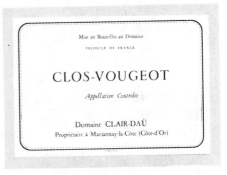

des Vougeot (white wine only), Clos de la Perrière, Les Cras, Les Petits Vougeots.

It is interesting to note that there are more than sixty owners of the Clos de Vougeot, each of whom has a plot of land within the vineyard. Many of these owners will sell their wine to different shippers, who in turn bottle it as "Clos de Vougeot."

CÔTE DE BEAUNE

The Côte de Beaune district produces some very fine red wine, softer than the reds of the CÔTE DE NUITS, and several outstanding white wines. Like the Côte de Nuits, the Côte de Beaune is divided into COMMUNES, which are further divided into *climats* or particular vineyards. Its red wines are somewhat less expensive than those of the Côte de Nuits, but one must still pay above-average prices for wines with famous communal appellations like ALOXE-CORTON or POMMARD. Some of the better buys are to be found in the less familiar communes of PERNAND-VERGELESSES, AUXEY-DURESSES, SAINT-ROMAIN, MONTHELIE, and SANTENAY. The red wines of CHASSAGNE-MONTRACHET (a commune also noted for excellent white wines) are available at reasonable prices as well.

The Côte de Beaune comprises the southern portion of the Côte d'Or (Golden Slope—the Côte de Nuits and the Côte de Beaune together make up the Côte d'Or) and extends from the commune of Ladoix-Serrigny in the north to the commune of Santenay in the south. The two noble grapes of Burgundy, the PINOT NOIR and the CHARDONNAY, are the most important red and white grapes of the Côte de Beaune.

Aloxe-Corton   Excellent red and white wines are produced in this COMMUNE. A wine simply labeled "Aloxe-Corton" will probably be of very good quality, but, as is the case with other communal appellations of Burgundy, it will often be rather expensive. Price comparisons will show that it is sometimes much wiser to buy a wine from one of the officially designated vineyards of the Aloxe-Corton commune such as Corton, Corton-Charlemagne (white), Basses-Mourettes, Bressandes, Les Chaillots, Les Chaumes, Clos du Roi, Les Fiètres, Les Four-

nières, Les Grèves, Les Guérets, Les Languettes, Les Maréchaudes, Les Meix, En Pauland, Les Perrières, Les Pougets, Les Renardes, Les Valozières, Les Vercots, La Vigne au Saint. The Corton is considered by most to be the greatest red wine of the Côte de Beaune.

Auxey-Duresses   With the price of Burgundy as high as it is, the moderately priced red and white wines of Auxey-Duresses

are a welcome relief. They are of good quality and are available in most well-stocked wine shops. The white Auxey-Duresses is a particularly good value at less than $5.00 a bottle. The First Growth (Premier Cru) vineyards include Les Bas des Duresses, Les Bretterins (or La Chapelle), Climat-du-Val (or Clos du Val), Les Duresses, Les Ecusseaux, Les Grands Champs, Reugne.

Bâtard-Montrachet (see CHASSAGNE-MONTRACHET)

Beaune The COMMUNE of Beaune produces mostly light red wines, all of which are very good, and a small quantity of fine dry white wine. The principal vineyards of the commune are Les Aigrots, Les Avaux, Les Blanches Fleurs, Les Boucherottes, Les Bressandes, Les Cent Vignes, Champs Pimont, Les Choua-cheux, Le Clos des Mouches, Le Clos de la Mousse, Clos du Roi, Aux Coucherias, Aux Cras, A l'Ecu, Les Epenottes, Les

131

Fèves, En Genêt, Les Grèves, Les Marconnets, La Mignotte, Montée Rouge, Les Montrevenots, En l'Orme, Les Perrières, Pertuisots, Les Reversées, Les Sisies, Les Teurons, Tiélandry (Clos Landry), Les Toussaints, Les Vignes Franches.

Côte de Beaune-Villages
A district appellation, very general in nature. Wines called Côte de Beaune-Villages come from certain COMMUNES within the Côte de Beaune but not from Beaune itself. These wines can be quite good, but they are often overpriced. One should not pay more than $5.00 for a Côte de Beaune-Villages. These are red wines only.

Chassagne-Montrachet
The COMMUNE of Chassagne produces some superb but expensive dry white wine and very good, affordable red wine. White wines that have only the Chassagne-Montrachet appellation and no vineyard name can be excellent values. When looking for a reasonably priced *red* wine of above-average quality, try the Chassagne.

The finest *climats* (vineyards) of Chassagne are BÂTARD-MONTRACHET, Criots-Bâtard-Montrachet, LE MONTRACHET (considered to be the best), Abbaye de Morgeot, La Boudriotte, En Cailleret, Les Champs Gain, Les Chenevottes, Clos Saint Jean, Les Grandes Ruchottes, Les Macherelles, La Maltroie, Morgeot, La Romanée, Les Vergers. The Grand Cru vineyards of Bâtard-Montrachet, Criots-Bâtard-Montrachet, and Le Montrachet have their own appellations. The remaining Premier Cru vineyards will have the commune name "Chassagne-Montrachet" on the label along with their own vineyard name.

133

Hospices de Beaune   In the heart of the city of Beaune sits the Hôtel Dieu, a gothic-style structure with oaken woodwork and a magnificent roof of brightly colored varnished tiles. It was built in the fifteenth century, and its construction vividly displays the influence of the Flemish architecture of that period. The Hôtel Dieu was founded by Nicolas Rolin in 1443, as a hospital for the poor. The term "Les Hospices de Beaune" encompasses the Hôtel Dieu and the building known as L'Hospice de la Charité de Beaune (The Hospital of Charity).

In order to maintain these institutions, the wine from the Hospices' vineyard holdings was sold each year. Beginning in the nineteenth century the wine was sold at public auction. The auction is traditionally held on the third Sunday in November, and most of the wine is sold to shippers who bottle it under their own Hospices de Beaune label. In addition to carrying the words "Hospices de Beaune," the label will have either a communal or a vineyard appellation, and the name of

the wine's *cuvée*. Since the vineyards are donated, the wine made from a specific parcel of land will bear the name of the individual who gave that land to the Hospices or the name of some other generous benefactor. The name of that person is designated as the *cuvée*. Some of the more famous *cuvées* are Nicolas Rolin (red wine from the COMMUNE of BEAUNE), Charlotte Dumay (red wine from the commune of ALOXE-CORTON), Rousseau-Deslandes (red wine from the commune of Beaune), Boillot (red wine from the commune of AUXEY-DURESSES), Docteur Peste (red wine from the commune of Aloxe-Corton), François de Salins (white wine from Meursault-Charmes), Philippe le Bon (white wine from Meursault-Genevrières), Maurice Drouhin (red wine from Beaune). Hospices de Beaune wines are always expensive because of their prestige and excellent quality.

Le Montrachet (see CHASSAGNE-MONTRACHET and PULIGNY-MONTRACHET)

Meursault
The white Meursault does not quite attain the distinction of the best MONTRACHETs, but it is an excellent dry wine nonetheless. The most expensive Meursaults will have the name of a *climat* (vineyard) on the label. The Premier Cru vineyards of the COMMUNE are Les Bouchères, Les Caillerets, Les Charmes Dessous, Les Charmes Dessus, Les Cras, Les Genevrières Dessous, Les Genevrières Dessus, La Goutte d'Or, La Jennelotte, Aux Perrières, Les Perrières Dessous, Les Per-

CHATEAU DE MEURSAULT

APPELLATION MEURSAULT CONTRÔLÉE

Propriété de M. le Comte de Moucheron

Mise du Domaine

ESTATE BOTTLED BY
COMTE DE MOUCHERON
CHATEAU DE MEURSAULT, CÔTE-D'OR

rières Dessus, Les Petures, La Pièce sous le Bois, Le Poruzot, Les Poruzots Dessus, Les Santenots Blancs, Les Santenots du Milieu, Sous le Dos d'Âne.

Monthelie   This COMMUNE produces good, reasonably priced red wine, not often seen in wine shops. The best vineyards of the commune are Le Cas Rougeot, Les Champs Fulliot, Le Château Gaillard, Le Clos Gauthey, Duresses, Sur Lavelle, Le Meix-Bataille, Les Riottes, La Taupine, Les Vignes Rondes.

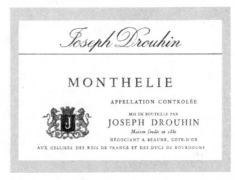

Pernand-Vergelesses The fruity red wines with the Pernand-Vergelesses appellation are often excellent values because of the relative anonymity of this COMMUNE. The better examples of Pernand-Vergelesses come from the following vineyards: Les Basses Vergelesses, En Caradeux, Creux de la Net, Les Fichots, Ile des Vergelesses. Fine quality and moderate price make Pernand-Vergelesses a very attractive wine buy.

Pommard The red wines of Pommard can be quite good, provided that they come from the better First Growth vineyards of the COMMUNE. Vineyard names to look for include Les Bertins, Les Boucherottes, Les Chanlins Bas, La Chanière, Les Chaponnières, Les Charmots, Clos Blanc, Clos de la Com-

maraine, Le Clos Micot, Clos du Verger, Les Combes Dessus, Les Croix Noires, Derrière Saint Jean, Les Epenots, Les Fremiers, Les Garollières, Les Pézerolles, La Platière, Les Poutures, La Refène, Les Rugiens, Les Sausilles.

Puligny-Montrachet The name of this COMMUNE is synonymous with outstanding dry white wine. Puligny-Montrachet produces elegant wines that even the least knowledgeable of wine drinkers can appreciate. The *climats* (vineyards) respon-

PULIGNY-MONTRACHET

APPELLATION CONTROLÉE

REMOISSENET PÈRE & FILS

NÉGOCIANTS-ÉLEVEURS A BEAUNE, COTE-D'OR, FRANCE

Joseph Drouhin

PRODUIT DE FRANCE
WHITE BURGUNDY TABLE WINE

CONTENTS - 1 PINT 8 FL. OZS.
ALCOHOL BY VOLUME 13% %

Montrachet

APPELLATION CONTROLÉE

Marquis de Laguiche

MONOPOLE : JOSEPH DROUHIN, NEGOCIANT A BEAUNE, COTE-D'OR

AGENT Dreyfus Ashby & Co NEW YORK, N.Y.

BURGUNDY
WHITE WINE
PRODUCT
OF FRANCE

FREDERICK
WILDMAN
AND SONS
NEW YORK CITY

CONTENTS
1 PT. 8 FL. OZS.
ALCOHOL
13.5% BY VOLUME

1973

Mis en bouteilles
à la Propriété

Bâtard-Montrachet

APPELLATION CONTROLÉE

DOMAINE LEFLAIVE
PROPRIÉTAIRE A PULIGNY-MONTRACHET (COTE-D'OR)

ALCOHOL 13.3 BY VOL.

Bienvenue-Bâtard-Montrachet

APPELLATION CONTROLÉE

1973
MISE AU DOMAINE

Étienne Sauzet
Propriétaire à Puligny-Montrachet (Côte-d'Or)

1970

Chevalier-Montrachet

"LES DEMOISELLES"
APPELLATION CHEVALIER-MONTRACHET CONTROLÉE

Mis en bouteilles à la propriété
LOUIS LATOUR, Négociant à Beaune (Côte-d'Or)

Joseph Drouhin

WHITE BURGUNDY TABLE WINE   ALCOHOL BY VOLUME 13%   CONTENTS 1 PINT 8 FLUID OZS.

PULIGNY-MONTRACHET
« CLOS DU CAILLERET »
APPELLATION CONTROLÉE

MIS EN BOUTEILLE PAR
JOSEPH DROUHIN
Maison fondée en 1880
NEGOCIANT A BEAUNE, COTE-D'OR
AUX CELLIERS DES ROIS DE FRANCE ET DES DUCS DE BOURGOGNE

AGENT Dreyfus Ashby & Co NEW YORK, N.Y.
PRODUCE OF FRANCE

GRANDS VINS DE BOURGOGNE

Puligny-Montrachet
Les Combettes
Appellation Contrôlée

Étienne Sauzet
Propriétaire à Puligny-Montrachet (Côte-d'Or)
Mise en bouteilles à la Propriété

139

sible for the great fame of MONTRACHET wines are Le Montrachet, Bâtard-Montrachet, Bienvenue-Bâtard-Montrachet, Chevalier-Montrachet. These are the Grand Cru (Great Growth) vineyards of the commune and the most expensive of the Montrachets. The less expensive Premier Crus (First Growths) vineyards of Puligny include Le Cailleret, Les Chalumeaux, Le Champ Canet, Clavoillons, Les Combettes, Les Folatières, La Garenne, Hameau de Blagny, Les Pucelles, Les Referts, Sous le Puits.

Saint Romain   The red and white wines of this little-known Burgundian COMMUNE should generally cost between $3.00 and $4.00. These are not wines of great distinction, but they are certainly drinkable and the price is right. Saint Romain wines are a rarity in most wine shops.

Santenay   The red wines from the better vineyards of the COMMUNE can be quite good. Wines that have no vineyard name on

140

the label are of questionable quality. The finest vineyards of Santenay are Beauregard, Beaurepaire, Clos de Tavannes, La Comme, Les Gravières, La Maladière, Le Passe-Temps.

Savigny-les-Beaune

The light red wines with the Savigny appellation (not found in great quantity in this country) should be consumed when fairly young. The First Growth vineyards of Savigny-les-Beaune are Basses Vergelesses, Bataillière, Les Charnières, Aux Clous, La Dominode, Aux Fourneaux, Aux Grands Liards, Aux Gravains, Aux Guettes, Les Hauts Jarrons, Les Hauts Marconnets, Les Lavières, Les Marconnets, Les Narbantons, Petits Godeaux, Aux Petits Liards, Les Peuillets, Redrescuts, Les Rouvrettes, Aux Serpentières, Les Talmettes, Aux Vergelesses.

Volnay The red wines of Volnay are smooth and delicate in taste when at their best. The finest examples come from the following First Growth vineyards: Les Angles, Les Aussy, La Barre (or Clos de la Barre), La Bousse d'Or (or La Pousse d'Or), Les Brouillards, En Caillerets, Caillerets-Dessus, Carelles-Dessous, Carelles sous la Chapelle, En Champans, Chanlin, En Chevret, Clos des Chênes, Clos des Ducs, Frémiets, Les Lurets, Les Mitans, En l'Ormeau, Les Petures, Pitures Dessus, Pointe d'Angles, Robardelle, Ronceret, Les Santenots, Taille-Pieds, En Verseuil, Village de Volnay.

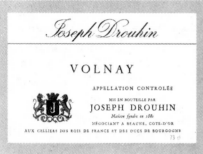

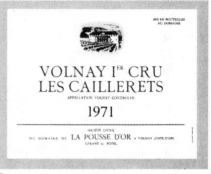

CHALONNAIS

The COMMUNES of RULLY, MERCUREY, GIVRY, and MONTAGNY constitute the wine district known as the Côte Chalonnaise. The red and white wines produced here are generally of good quality and not very expensive. These are not Burgundy's best wines, but they can make pleasant drinking in good years. With the exception of the red Mercurey, most of the other wines from the Chalonnais will not always be easy to find in American wine shops.

Givry   Red wines with the Givry appellation and no vineyard name will be reasonably priced (less then $5.00). Wines with vineyard names on the label will probably be somewhat more expensive. Some of the more famous vineyards of the COMMUNE include Le Cellier aux Moines, Clos Saint Paul, Clos Saint Pierre, Clos Salomon.

Mercurey   The red Mercurey has body and originality and is not as expensive as many of the red wines of the CÔTE DE BEAUNE and CÔTE DE NUITS. Certain examples of the Mercurey can be quite expensive, sometimes going as high as $8.00. The better values lie in the $6.00-and-less price range. Some good vineyards include Les Fourneaux, Clos Marcilly, Clos de Myglands, Clos du Roi, Les Voyens.

Montagny Dry, light white wine made from the CHARDONNAY grape dominates in this COMMUNE. It can be quite good but is hardly of the same caliber as the better white wines of the CÔTE DE BEAUNE or the MÂCONNAIS.

Rully This COMMUNE produces mostly white wine, but some red wine can also be found. Rully is particularly famous for its sparkling wine.

MÂCONNAIS

The Mâcon district of southern Burgundy is noted for its very fine dry white wines made from the Chardonnay grape. This area should be explored by all wine lovers who are looking for moderately priced white wines of above-average quality. I have tasted some very nice wines with the simple Pinot-Chardonnay Mâcon

144

or Mâcon-Villages appellations that cost less than $3.00. Of course wine from the COMMUNES of POUILLY-FUISSÉ, POUILLY-LOCHÉ, and POUILLY-VINZELLES will be more expensive, the Pouilly-Fuissé sometimes reaching as high as $7.00 or $8.00 a bottle. But even so, there are enough good, inexpensive wines from Mâcon to satisfy the quality-minded wine buyer. Provided that the wine being purchased is from a good shipper or vineyard owner, and that it is of a good year, the Mâcon wine experience can be most rewarding.

Mâcon Red and white wines are entitled to the simple Mâcon appellation, but some of the best values are to be found in white wines with the Mâcon, Mâcon Supérieur, Mâcon-Villages, and Pinot Chardonnay-Mâcon appellations. Wines of the Mâcon-Villages category may use the name of the COMMUNE of origin on the label like Mâcon-Vire or Mâcon- Lugny.

Pouilly-Fuissé

The Pouilly-Fuissé is a crisp and flavorful dry white wine of distinction, perhaps the best white wine of the Mâcon district. Unfortunately, the better bottles will sell for about $8.00.

Pouilly-Loché, Pouilly-Vinzelles

The white wines produced in the COMMUNES of Fuissé, Loché, and Vinzelles are all similar in taste and style, but POUILLY-FUISSÉ is the acknowledged king. The very good Pouilly-Loché and Pouilly-Vinzelles make fine, less expensive substitutes.

Saint Veran   The Saint Veran is a good dry white wine that is similar to those wines with the Mâcon-Villages appellation. The low price tag (less than $4.00) makes the Saint Veran a very attractive buy.

BEAUJOLAIS

Beaujolais, the southernmost wine district of Burgundy, produces a very large quantity of light, fruity red wine that must be consumed when young and is at its best when served slightly chilled. It is a delightfully thirst-quenching wine that has become quite popular over the past few years because of its generally good quality and moderate price. In addition, Beaujolais is an easy wine to drink. It is not harsh and tannic, like many of the young red wines of Burgundy and BORDEAUX, but is full of fruit and smooth when well made. But beware: Poorly vinified Beaujolais, or Beaujolais that is past its prime, can be very offensive. The purchaser should therefore choose only those bottles with the names of reputable Burgundian shippers or vineyard owners on the label and only buy young Beaujolais—a four-year-old bottle is already past its prime.

Beaujolais, Beaujolais Supérieur, Beaujolais-Villages   These are the three basic appellations for Beaujolais wines. Beaujolais-Villages is the best of the three, because the grapes used to produce wines with this appellation

147

come from some of the better vineyards of the Beaujolais district. These wines may also carry the name of a COMMUNE on the label such as Saint-Amour-Bellevue or Emeringes.

Beaujolais de l'Année (see BEAUJOLAIS NOUVEAU)

Beaujolais Blanc (White Beaujolais)　A small quantity of dry white Beaujolais made from the CHARDONNAY grape is produced in the district. It resembles the white wines of neighboring MÂCON.

Beaujolais Nouveau (New Beaujolais) The name "Beaujolais Nouveau" is given to the first wine of the year from the Beaujolais district, made almost immediately after the September harvest. The grapes are rapidly crushed and the juice is left in wood for about a month prior to bottling. This procedure allows the wine to retain the naturally fresh and fruity characteristics of the GAMAY NOIR grape, but it must be consumed as soon as it appears on the market. After only a few months Beaujolais Nouveau loses its freshness and is no longer drinkable.

November 15 is the traditional arrival date in Paris for this young wine, and the French always drink it up with extraordinary enthusiasm. Most cafés buy small casks of Beaujolais Nouveau and serve it directly to their customers. Even though the bottled Beaujolais Nouveau found in this country bears little resemblance to the delicious cask wine that can be sampled in Parisian cafés, it is a unique and satisfying light red wine that is worthy of consideration. But remember that Beaujolais Nouveau is best when very young, so do not buy a bottle if it

is more than six months old. The methods of vinification are such that the youth and fruitiness of this wine will only be lost with the onset of time.

Since it is not advisable to save Beaujolais Nouveau, a list of the best vintages would be misleading. We can only say, drink it each year and judge the quality for youself. It should cost about $3.00. The expressions BEAUJOLAIS PRIMEUR and BEAU-JOLAIS DE L'ANNÉE are synonymous with Beaujolais Nouveau.

Beaujolais Primeur (see BEAUJOLAIS NOUVEAU)

Beaujolais Supérieur (see BEAUJOLAIS)

Beaujolais-Villages (see BEAUJOLAIS)

Brouilly (see CRUS)

Chénas (see CRUS)

Côte de Brouilly (see CRUS)

Crus
The very best wines of Beaujolais are designated as the crus (growths). These wines are more substantial than the other Beaujolais and, when from good years, can last for some time. There are nine crus, each one having its own appellation: Brouilly, Côte de Brouilly, Chenás, Chiroubles, Fleurie, Julienas, Morgon, Moulin-à-Vent, Saint Amour. A few of these crus, particularly Moulin-à-Vent, can be given four or five years before being consumed, unlike lesser Beaujolais, which must be drunk before the age of two or three.

Chiroubles
Château de Javernand
Appellation Chiroubles Contrôlée
MÉDAILLES D'OR 1973 ET 1975
JEAN FOURNEAU
PROPRIÉTAIRE-RÉCOLTANT A CHIROUBLES (RHÔNE)
73 cl

1973
Château des Labourons
APPELLATION FLEURIE CONTRÔLÉE

COMTE B. DE LESCURE
PROPRIÉTAIRE-RÉCOLTANT A FLEURIE (RHÔNE)
DISTRIBUÉ PAR
LE CONCESSIONNAIRE
FAYE NÉGOCIANT-ÉLEVEUR A MACON (S&L) FRANCE
CONTENTS 1 PINT 8 FL. OZ.
ALCOHOL 12% BY VOLUME
PRODUIT DE FRANCE

GEORGES DUBŒUF
JULIÉNAS
APPELLATION CONTROLÉE
LES VINS GEORGES DUBŒUF A ROMANÈCHE-THORINS .71
0,75 L.

FONDÉE EN 1859
MORGON
APPELLATION CONTROLÉE
PRODUCED AND BOTTLED BY
LOUIS JADOT
WINE GROWER AT BEAUNE (COTE-D'OR) FRANCE

PRODUCE OF FRANCE
ALC. BY VOL. 13.1%
3/4 QUART
RED BURGUNDY
TABLE WINE
IMPORTED BY KOBRAND CORPORATION, N.Y., N.Y., SOLE U.S. IMPORTERS

MISE EN BOUTEILLES AU DOMAINE
Moulin-à-Vent
Appellation Contrôlée
Les Combes
JEAN-PIERRE BLOUD ROMANÈCHE-THORINS, S.-&-L.

RED BURGUNDY TABLE WINE
ALCOHOL 13% BY VOLUME
IMPORTED BY CHATEAU AND ESTATE WINES
DIVISION OF BROWNE VINTNERS, NEW YORK, N.Y.
NET CONTENTS 1 PINT 8 FL. OZ.
PRODUCE OF FRANCE

Joseph Drouhin
SAINT-AMOUR
APPELLATION CONTROLÉE
MIS EN BOUTEILLE PAR
JOSEPH DROUHIN
Maison fondée en 1880
NÉGOCIANT A BEAUNE, COTE-D'OR
AUX CELLIERS DES ROIS DE FRANCE ET DES DUCS DE BOURGOGNE
75 cl

Champagne

France could not have done more to enhance her own international prestige than when she appointed the wines of Champagne as her goodwill ambassadors. For years the bubbly has been an integral part of festivities in the United States and the world over. Whenever we think of weddings, birthdays, anniversaries, and graduations, we are inevitably led to thoughts of the delicious effervescent wine from the province of Champagne. There have been many attempts to imitate this wine, but no one has succeeded in duplicating it. Only the province of Champagne has the proper soil and climate to bring the PINOT NOIR, CHARDONNAY, and Pinot Meunier grapes to their perfection; and only French wine makers have the technical knowledge and experience to process and blend these grapes so that they may yield the fine sparkling wine that has become a symbol of gaiety and good living.

Because of the extreme care given Champagne, it will never be an inexpensive wine. The grapes used are the finest and production methods are unhurried. It takes time to make a good Champagne. There are several steps in the making of this wine, and each one is of great importance. After the grapes have been crushed, the juice is collected and placed in casks or vats for fermentation. The wine that results from this first fermentation is nonsparkling. When the wine is ready, the important task of blending begins. The various districts of Champagne yield grapes of differing characteristics and quality.

Fully aware of this fact, Champagne houses try to create a satisfying blend of wine from these districts in order to obtain the traditional style associated with their particular brand of Champagne. Unless the year is a superior one, only nonvintage Champagne will be made. This means that during the blending process, "reserve" wines from past vintages are added to the wine just fermented. These reserve wines usually come from superior vintages, so their addition to the blend will complement the qualities of the new wine. Blending is perhaps the most important step in making Champagne because it is at this time that the wine is given its character and individuality. Only expert wine makers and tasters can marry the qualities found in the old and new wines. The wine that results from this blending is called the *cuvée*.

In exceptional years, vintage Champagne is made. A vintage Champagne is composed of wine from one particular year. The extensive blending of old and new wine that takes place for the production of a nonvintage Champagne is not necessary because the qualities of the new wine are outstanding on their own. Vintage Champagne will always have a year marked on the label and, due to its superior quality, is more expensive than nonvintage Champagne.

After the composition of the house blend (*cuvée*), the wine is ready for a second fermentation, which will take place in the bottle. Before bottling, however, the wine is given a small amount of sugar and yeast in order to cause the second fermentation. It is this step that will give the Champagne its sparkle. The sugar, combined with some old wine, is called the "Liqueur de Tirage." When the wine and liqueur are left in a sealed bottle for the proper length of time, the formation of carbonic gas results. It is this gas that is responsible for the many bubbles we see in Champagne. Once the wine has been bottled, it is left in the cellar to age. A minimum of one year is required for nonvintage Champagne, three years for vintage Champagne.

During the second fermentation, sediment forms in the bottle. The process of removing the sediment begins while the bottles are

154

still in the cellar. Each bottle is placed neck down in what is called a *pupitre* (desk), a wooden rack containing many holes. The man known as the *remueur* tilts the bottle slightly downward each day in order to coax the sediment into the neck. By the time he is finished, the bottle is completely perpendicular. When the sediment is ready to be removed, the bottles are transferred to a conveyor belt and plunged into a freezing liquid, in such a way that only the neck of the bottle is immersed. This procedure freezes the sediment in a block of ice and allows it to be easily ejected from the bottle when the capsule is removed. The process of removing the sediment is called *dégorgement* or disgorging.

When the expulsion of the ice and sediment is complete, some old Champagne and sugar (known as the Liqueur d'Expédition) is added. This addition serves a twofold purpose. First, it fills the gap that is left when the sediment is disgorged, because some wine is lost in this step. Second, it gives the Champagne a particular degree of sweetness. The amount of sugar that is added depends upon the type of wine desired. There is very dry Champagne that receives virtually no sugar, called brut; slightly sweeter Champagne known as extra-dry; and rather sweet Champagne called sec (dry), demi-sec (half-dry), and doux (sweet). One of these words will be found on a Champagne label. The very dry brut Champagne is generally considered to be the best type of wine because the lack of sweetness permits the true qualities of the grapes to display themselves. A brut Champagne is very difficult to make due to the fact that defects are more easily detectable when there is less sugar in the wine. Sweet Champagne can mask technical faults and poor quality.

The combination of sugar and old wine that is added to new wine is called the Liqueur d'Expédition because this is one of the last steps before the wine is sent on its way (expedited) to importers and retailers. The process of sweetening the Champagne to the required degree is called the *dosage*. After completion of the *dosage*, the bottles are ready for corking and dressing. The special Champagne cork and wire muzzle create an airtight seal so that the gas cannot escape, then the label and decorative foil are added. The Champagne is now ready for distribution to all parts of the world.

156

When shopping for Champagne, one should be concerned with the names of the different Champagne firms, because they are responsible for making the wine. Usually they will buy their grapes from independent growers, crush them, and produce the wine. Virtually all of the Champagnes exported to this country are excellent, but they do differ in style. Some are on the light side, others are more full-bodied. By experimenting with the different brands of Champagne and the varying degrees of sweetness, you will discover the style of wine that suits your personal preference. The inordinately pleasurable task of tasting is the only valid method of discovering those characteristics that you enjoy in a Champagne. The best Champagne houses exporting wine to the United States include:

Ayala
Bollinger
Canard-Duchêne
Charbaut
Charles Heidsieck
de Castellane
Deutz & Geldermann
Heidsieck Monopole
Krug
Lanson Père et Fils
Laurent Perrier

Louis Roederer
Moët et Chandon
G. H. Mumm
Perrier-Jouet
Piper-Heidsieck
Pol Roger
Pommery-Greno
Ruinart Père et Fils
Taittinger
Veuve Clicquot-Ponsardin

Due to the high cost of fine grapes, the painstaking techniques involved in making Champagne, and high import taxes on sparkling wine, good Champagne will never be inexpensive. A nonvintage Champagne will cost between $8.00 and $13.00, whereas vintage Champagne will be closer to $16.00. BLANC DE BLANCS Champagnes and other special bottlings often fetch much higher prices (see labels of special bottlings that follow). The Champagne firm of A. Charbaut et Fils produces very drinkable and less expensive wine. Their vintage Champagne sells for about $9.99; the nonvintage costs about $8.99.

Champagne Vintages

Only the best years are suitable for making vintage Champagne. Most of the wine produced is nonvintage and will not carry a specific year on the label. Recent vintage years include 1966, 1969, 1970, 1971, 1973, 1976.

Champagne is best when consumed young, although some vintage Champagnes have lasted for many years. It is advisable to drink this wine as soon as you buy it, rather than allowing it to "age" in your cellar, because Champagnes no longer improve after disgorgement. Do not buy a bottle of vintage Champagne if it is more than seven years old.

Blanc de Blancs This expression is of great significance when discussing the wines of Champagne. Only those wines made from the white CHARDONNAY grape may use the expres-

sion on their label, because Blanc de Blancs (literally "white of whites") means "white wine made from white grapes."

A Blanc de Blancs wine is lighter and more delicate than wine that is composed of a blend of white and black grapes, but this does not necessarily mean that it is better. Let your taste buds decide. Most Champagne is made from a blend of PINOT NOIR (black), CHARDONNAY (white), and a small percentage of Pinot Meunier (black) grapes. A Blanc de Blancs Champagne is usually more expensive than a regular Champagne.

Bouzy   Few people are aware that still (nonsparkling) red wine is produced in the province of Champagne in addition to the traditional sparkling white wine. The village of Bouzy makes an excellent light red wine from the PINOT NOIR grape. The Bouzy is usually made by individual growers within the district, and not by the large Champagne houses. Unfortunately, the local inhabitants tend to keep this wine for themselves, making the supply of Bouzy in the United States rather limited. The Bouzy has a CÔTEAUX CHAMPENOIS controlled appellation.

Champagne

The laws governing the production of sparkling Champagne are probably the strictest of all French wine laws. The shopper might be surprised to find that the words "Appellation Contrôlée" do not appear on labels of sparkling wine. This is so because the word "Champagne" on the label serves as a controlled appellation in itself. Only those wines produced within the delimited area of Champagne and according to traditional methods are entitled to call themselves Champagne. This word, along with the name of a good firm, is your guarantee that the wine is authentic and of a high quality. In addition to sparkling white wine, some firms also make Champagne Rosé. The same high standards of production apply to both types of wine.

Côteaux Champenois

This is an appellation given to both red and white still (nonsparkling) wines from the province of Champagne. The words "Côteaux Champenois" (Champagne Slopes) make it clear that the wine is not the more famous

sparkling Champagne, for only sparkling white or rosé wine may bear the sole word "Champagne" on the label.

Most of the wine produced under the Côteaux Champenois appellation is white and is made from the CHARDONNAY grape. The red BOUZY, made from the PINOT NOIR grape, also carries this appellation. Some of the major Champagne firms produce the dry, white still wines: Bollinger, A. Charbaut, Laurent Perrier, and Moët et Chandon are four companies that have recently begun marketing them in this country.

Crémant   The word "crémant" (creaming) is used to describe those wines that are less effervescent than the standard sparkling Champagne. This is a wine to try while in France, because it will not, as a rule, be found in the United States.

162

Côtes du Rhône

The Côtes du Rhône (Rhône Slopes) wine region is located in southeastern France. The vineyards begin in Vienne, just south of Lyon, and follow the Rhône River on its southerly course as far as Avignon, in Provence. This 120-mile stretch produces quite a variety of wines: robust reds, strong dry white wines, sweet and grapey white sparkling wines, and very dry rosés. These are wines of high quality and many are reasonably priced. There are some excellent red, white, and rosé wines available in this country for less than $5.00, a true bargain in today's world of inflated wine prices.

Certain Rhône Valley wines are noted for their high alcoholic content, particularly the red CHÂTEAUNEUF-DU-PAPE, which sometimes attains 14 percent. Wines from the CÔTE RÔTIE and HERMITAGE vineyards are also known for their full-bodied vigor. Some of these red wines are quite coarse when young but become much smoother as they mature. Generally the bigger red wines of the Rhône Valley age well, as do some of the white wines.

The Rhône Valley is a unique and interesting area for several reasons. We have seen that most French wine regions grow only a few different types of grapes, usually no more than three or four. The Rhône Valley vineyard breaks with this trend, because it contains about twenty different grape varieties, all of which thrive in the warm climate and varied soils of the region. The grapes of the Rhône include Syrah, GRENACHE, Viognier, Cinsault, Mourvèdre, Clairette, Picpoul, Roussanne, Marsanne, Terret Noir, Picardan, Bourboulenc, Carignan, MUSCAT, Counoise, Vaccarese, Muscardin, Ungi Blanc, Maccabéo, Calidor.

When shopping for Rhône Valley wines one should be aware of the different kinds of appellations that exist. The Côtes du Rhône appellation is a very general one; it tells the buyer that the wine is good but is not among the best wines of the Rhône.

One step above the simple Côtes du Rhône appellation is Côtes du Rhône Villages. The best wines of this category will have the name of a village on the label like Côtes du Rhône-Chusclan or Côtes du Rhône-Vacqueyras. These will be better values than wines that say only Côtes du Rhône Villages.

The very best Rhône Valley wines have their own local appellations such as CHÂTEAUNEUF-DU-PAPE, HERMITAGE, CROZES-HERMITAGE, CÔTE RÔTIE, TAVEL, and will not bear the words "Côtes du Rhône" as part of the appellation. These wines come from specific COMMUNES and are not blended with wines coming from other areas within the Rhône Valley, as is the case with a simple Côtes du Rhône wine. Another reason for the fine quality of communal wines is that the vineyards producing them are much smaller than the vineyards entitled to produce wines calling themselves Côtes du Rhône. This limited growing area adds substantially to the overall quality of the wine.

Côtes du Rhône Vintages

Good years for the red wines of the Rhône Valley are 1967 (excellent), 1969, 1970 (excellent), 1971, 1972, 1974, and 1976. The big red wines of the Rhône like HERMITAGE, CÔTE RÔTIE, and CHÂTEAUNEUF-DU-PAPE should not be consumed before they are five or six years old. When young these wines tend to be harsh, but aging will soften them considerably. White, rosé, and lesser red wines from the Rhône should be drunk while they are young—from one to three years old.

Château Grillet   This is probably the best white wine of the Rhône. It is also extremely rare. Château Grillet is a very flavorful dry white wine but is quite expensive when found in the United States. A visitor to the Rhône Valley would do well to look for this wine in the superb restaurants of the region, or in a wine shop.

Châteauneuf-du-Pape   The village of Châteauneuf-du-Pape (New Castle of the Pope) produces one of the best and most famous red wines of the Rhône. It is high in alcohol, full-bodied, and distinctive. A very good bottle of Châteauneuf-

du-Pape will cost about $7.00, a reasonable price for a wine of quality. Some of the best vineyards of the COMMUNE are Château des Fines Roches, Château Fortia, Château de la Gardine, Château de la Nerthe, Château Rayas, Clos des Papes, Domaine de Mont Redon, Domaine de la Solitude. If one wants to be sure of receiving a fine example of a Châteauneuf-du-Pape, one will choose a wine with one of these vineyard names on the label. Ultimately, it will be the best value. A small amount of dry white Châteauneuf-du-Pape is also made.

Clairette de Die   The Rhône Valley is a land steeped in history, and nothing reveals this tradition more than the wine called Clairette de Die. It seems that this wine, from the village of Die on the Drôme River (an effluent of the Rhône), was very popular with Roman emperors and noblemen. It is a sparkling white wine made from the Clairette and MUSCAT grapes. The perfumed and flowery qualities of the wine, com-

bined with its effervescence, make the Clairette de Die one of the more original and unusual wines of the Rhône Valley. This is a wine to sample when in France, because little, if any, will be found in this country.

Condrieu   This rare dry white wine is a close cousin to CHÂTEAU GRILLET. If you come across a bottle, it will most likely be very expensive. Like Château Grillet, Condrieu is made exclusively from the Viognier grape.

Cornas   The red Cornas is a somewhat coarse and earthy wine that needs time in the bottle to mature. One should wait until the wine is at least five to six years old before drinking it.

Côte Rôtie   This is one of the Rhône Valley's prestigious appellations. The red Côte Rôtie is a fruity, full-bodied wine

of excellent quality. Its best vineyards are Côte Brune and Côte Blonde. The Syrah and Viognier grapes produce the Côte Rôtie.

Côtes du Rhône This is the most general Rhône Valley appellation and applies to red, white, and rosé wines coming from designated COMMUNES within the entire Côtes du Rhône region. Wines with a Côtes du Rhône Villages appellation are usually of a higher quality, especially if the name of a specific

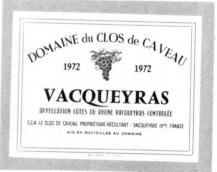

village is found on the label. Some village names to look for are Cairanne, Chusclan, Laudun, Vacqueyras. Wines from particular villages are generally more robust than those wines called simply Côtes du Rhône.

Crozes-Hermitage
Both red and white wines of fine quality are produced under this appellation. The wines of Crozes-Hermitage are not as distinguished as those with the HERMITAGE appellation, but they are a good value (less than $4.00).

Gigondas
The village of Gigondas is located in the south-eastern portion of the Rhône Valley, north of CHÂTEAUNEUF-DU-PAPE. Very good, sturdy red wines are made here, and they are a fine value if priced at less than $5.00.

Hermitage   The vineyards of Hermitage produce both red and white wines, but the reds are primarily responsible for the great fame that Hermitage has enjoyed over the years. The red wines are solid and full-bodied and can last for many years.

Some very fine dry white wine, made from the Marsanne and Roussanne grapes, is produced in Hermitage as well. Red Hermitage is made from the Syrah grape. The finest red wine vineyards of the area are Les Bressards, Le Méal, Greffieux. Chante-Alouette is the most famous white wine vineyard of Hermitage.

Wines with the Hermitage appellation on the label and no vineyard name can be excellent buys provided that they come from good Rhône Valley shippers.

Lirac   Red, white, and rosé wines are entitled to the Lirac appellation, but the dry rosés are the best known.

Saint Joseph   Most often one will see red wines carrying this appellation, though some white wine can also be found. The red Saint Joseph is a light and fruity wine of good quality and is available for $5.00 or less.

Saint Péray The wine called Saint Péray Mousseux is an excellent sparkling white wine made according to the traditional CHAMPAGNE method The nonsparkling dry white Saint Péray is more widely available and sells for less than $5.00.

Tavel Tavel is considered by many to be the best rosé produced in France. It is a dry, fruity (and sometimes heady) wine, made primarily from the GRENACHE grape. A good Tavel rosé can be purchased for about $5.00.

Wines of
the Loire Valley

The Loire Valley, situated about 100 miles south of Paris, is known for its delightful assortment of wines—mostly white and rosé—as well as for its array of medieval and renaissance châteaux that line the spacious Loire and Cher rivers. The wines of the region are as varied as the mood and architectural design of each château. Here one can find some of the driest white wines that France has to offer and, at the same time, several medium-dry and sweet wines. The valley is of particular interest to the wine lover because most of the wines found here are of high quality, show a great deal of originality, and are readily available in the United States at moderate prices. In addition, all Loire Valley wines can accompany meals or be savored by themselves.

The five most important wine-producing districts of the Loire Valley are POUILLY-SUR-LOIRE, SANCERRE, VOUVRAY, ANJOU, and Nantes, where the wine known as MUSCADET is produced.

In addition to knowing the significance of each of these wine districts, it is necessary to become familiar with the names of certain viticulteurs (wine growers) or négociants (shippers) who produce and/or bottle superior wine. After the words "Appellation Contrôlée," the name of the wine producer or shipper is your assurance that the wine you are about to purchase is a good one.

The years 1973, 1974, 1975, and 1976 are good years for the white wines of the Loire.

ANJOU

The ancient province of Anjou, in the western portion of the Loire Valley, is noted principally for its rosés. Like the VOUVRAY, the rosés from Anjou attain different degrees of sweetness based upon climate and methods of production. One can find the rosé sec (dry), demi-sec (half-dry), and doux (sweet).

Wines with the appellation Rosé d'Anjou are made from a combination of grapes including the CABERNET SAUVIGNON, Cabernet

Franc, Groslot, Pineau d'Aunis, GAMAY, and Cot, the last four being grapes of fair quality. The very good Cabernet d'Anjou is a rosé made exclusively from Cabernet grapes. It is drier and of a higher quality than the Rosé d'Anjou.

Anjou produces red, white, and rosé wines, but few reds are ever exported to the United States. Since the rosé is such a popular wine it often overshadows the very excellent sweet white wines produced in the CÔTEAUX DU LAYON district of Anjou. Wines from this area will have the Anjou appellation on their labels unless they come from one of the more prestigious crus like QUARTS-DE-CHAUME, which is entitled to its own appellation. These wines are among the sturdiest of all French wines because some can last for twenty years or more.

Note that the rosé and white wines discussed here are all in the Appellation Contrôlée category, but beware of rosés from France labeled under commercial names that attempt to imitate the Rosé d'Anjou but which have neither the AOC nor VDQS expression on their label. Such wines are subject to far fewer governmental controls than the true rosés from Anjou, and they are often overpriced.

Both the Rosé d'Anjou and Cabernet d'Anjou go well with simple light meals, and both can serve as refreshing summertime thirst quenchers. It is best to drink them while they are young (between one and three years old).

Côteaux de la Loire This area produces mostly white wines that tend to be drier than those from the CÔTEAUX DU LAYON district. Surrounding the village of Savennières (located within the Côteaux de la Loire) are some especially fine growths, the most famous being the COULÉE DE SERRANT.

Côteaux du Layon In this district of Anjou the CHENIN BLANC grape yields some very distinguished sweet white wines. During the better years the grapes are attacked by the Pourriture Noble (Noble Rot) enabling them to produce an even sweeter, more delectable wine similar to the great wines of SAUTERNES. The best areas are QUARTS-DE-CHAUME and Bonnezeaux.

Coulée de Serrant (see CÔTEAUX DE LA LOIRE)

Quarts-de-Chaume (see CÔTEAUX DU LAYON)

Saumur The wine known as Saumur Mousseux (Sparkling Saumur) is produced in the Saumur area of Anjou. It is a rather popular wine in France because it can serve as an inexpensive alternative to CHAMPAGNE. Saumur Mousseux is a wine of fair quality.

Savennières (see CÔTEAUX DE LA LOIRE)

MUSCADET

The vineyards that produce the very dry and fruity white Muscadet are found to the extreme west of the Loire Valley near Nantes (Brittany) at the mouth of the Loire River. It is here that the Melon de Bourgogne, the grape that produces the Muscadet, is most widely planted. In the Nantes area the Melon de Bourgogne is also called the Muscadet, making this one of the few districts of France that uses the grape as part of the name of the wine.

There are three Appellations Contrôlées for the Muscadet: (1) Muscadet de Sèvre et Maine, (2) Muscadet, and (3) Muscadet des Côteaux de la Loire. The first two are seen on many wine labels in this country, but the Muscadet de Sèvre et Maine appellation is considered to be the best because of superior soil and climatic conditions in the Sèvre et Maine area. Several fine bottles of the Muscadet de Sèvre et Maine may be purchased for less than $4.00. Within the Sèvre et Maine district there are a few COMMUNES noted

for their excellent Muscadet including Clisson, La Chappelle-Heulin, Gorges, Monnières, Le Pallet, La Regrippière, Saint-Fiacre-sur-Maine, Vallet, Vertou.

Muscadet should be consumed while it is young, ideally within one to three years of the vintage date. This wine goes well with fish of all kinds, but most Frenchmen seem to agree that the Muscadet best accompanies shellfish, especially fresh oysters.

Gros Plant du Pays Nantais This wine has the VDQS rating, the second highest category after the AOC. Like the Muscadet, the Gros Plant du Pays Nantais is named after the grape that produces it, the Gros Plant, more popularly known as the FOLLE BLANCHE. This grape is inferior to the MUSCADET, but it yields a pleasant dry white wine.

Mis(e) en Bouteilles sur Lie Literally means "bottled on sediment or deposit." Individual wine producers treat their MUSCADET differently after the grapes have been crushed. Many will filter their wine several times before bottling takes place in order to remove any sediment that has been picked up from the cask and from dead yeast cells. There are those wine producers, however, who believe that filtering a Muscadet will destroy its naturally fresh and fruity characteristics, so they prefer to draw the wine from the cask and bottle it while it is still in contact with the lees (sediment). This adds a greater dimension of flavor to the wine and helps to preserve its youth. The expression "Mis(e) en bouteilles sur lie" is generally an indication of a more flavorful wine. The method of bottling "sur lie" is not unique to the Muscadet, for several other white wines go through the same process, but it is in connection with this wine that the expression has gained recognition.

POUILLY-FUMÉ

The appellation Pouilly-Fumé refers to a dry white wine made from the SAUVIGNON BLANC grape, sometimes called the BLANC FUMÉ. When at its best, the Pouilly-Fumé is a wine of distinction—slightly spicy with a hint of "smoke," as the name implies ("fumé" means smoked). The second appellation that may be used on a label in place of Pouilly-Fumé is Blanc Fumé de Pouilly or Pouilly-Blanc-Fumé. This appellation does, however, refer to the same wine. A third appellation of the district that is not the same as the first two is POUILLY-SUR-LOIRE. A wine calling itself by this name is made from the Chasselas, a grape that does not attain the stature of the Sauvignon Blanc. Wines with the Pouilly-sur-Loire appellation are not exported in great quantity to the United States.

CHATEAU DE TRACY

APPELLATION POUILLY FUMÉ CONTROLÉE

COMTE A D'ESTUTT D'ASSAY
TRACY-SUR-LOIRE
(NIÈVRE)

MISE EN BOUTEILLE AU CHATEAU

A Pouilly-Fumé that does not come from a recognized vineyard will usually cost less than $5.00 but a wine that is considered to be from a superior vineyard will sometimes cost more than $7.00. Some of these better vineyards include Château du Nozet, Bascoins, Bernadats, loges, Château de Tracy.

Blanc Fumé   This is another name for the SAUVIGNON BLANC, the grape that produces the Pouilly-Fumé. One will sometimes see the words "Blanc Fumé de Pouilly" on a wine label instead of "Pouilly-Fumé," since both names are used to designate one and the same wine.

Pouilly-sur-Loire   An area in the southeastern corner of the Loire Valley, where the wine known as Pouilly-Fumé is produced. A Pouilly-sur-Loire appellation is inferior to a Pouilly-Fumé or Blanc Fumé de Pouilly appellation.

SANCERRE

The little village of Sancerre, situated on the west bank of the Loire River, directly faces POUILLY-SUR-LOIRE, which sits on the east bank. The excellent Sancerre is similar to the POUILLY-FUMÉ because it is white and is made from the same grape, the SAUVIGNON BLANC.

The Sancerre is slightly drier and somewhat less flavorful than the Pouilly-Fumé. The principal difference between the two wines is price: The Sancerre is usually less expensive than the often over-priced Pouilly-Fumé.

The Sancerre district also produces a small quantity of good red and rosé wines that rarely travel outside of France.

Chavignol   A commune within the larger district of Sancerre reputed to be one of the finest areas for the production of the white Sancerre. Chavignol possesses some outstanding small vineyards designated as crus or growths. Some of the better-known growths include Monts Damnés, Comtesse, Cul de Beaujeu. Even though these crus are not always readily available, the name "Chavignol" is frequently seen on the finer bottles of Sancerre.

   In addition to Chavignol, Amigny and Bué are two other villages known for their superior Sancerre.

Quincy   This town is a few miles to the southwest of Sancerre. Here, the SAUVIGNON BLANC produces a dry white wine, similar in character to the Sancerre. Since the vineyards of Quincy are quite small, one might have to go to France to find a bottle of this very good and inexpensive wine.

VOUVRAY

The white Vouvray can be one of the most interesting of all Loire Valley wines. Depending upon the climate and the method of production, it is dry (sec), half-dry (demi-sec), or sweet (doux).

182

Many people believe that Vouvray is best when it is on the sweet side, for this is when the flavor of honey, fruit, spice, and musk blend with each other to form a complex and delicious wine that can be enjoyed on its own as an apéritif, or with fruit as a dessert wine. A dry Vouvray best accompanies fish or white meats.

Besides the regular still (nonsparkling) Vouvray, some wine producers make what is called a Vouvray Mousseux, a sparkling wine usually made according to the traditional CHAMPAGNE method.

183

Both the still and the sparkling Vouvrays are very agreeable and inexpensive (less than $5.00).

The Vouvray is made from the CHENIN BLANC grape, also called the Pineau de la Loire. Some of the better vineyards of the district are Château de Moncontour, Clos de l'Auberdière, Clos de Vigneau, Clos le Mont, Clos du Bourg.

Bourgueil   The Cabernet Franc grape is responsible for this fruity red wine. Like the CHINON, the Bourgueil makes fine drinking, but is rarely found in the United States. This is by no means France's most distinguished red wine, but it is very good and inexpensive. The vineyards of Bourgueil are located near Chinon, in the central portion of the Loire Valley (Province of Touraine).

 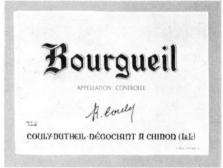

Chinon   The village of Chinon is located on the Vienne River several miles west of the Vouvray district. The red Chinon should be consumed when fairly young, up to four years after

the vintage date. This wine will not often be found in the United States, but it is a wine that should be tasted when visiting the Loire Valley. Chinon is an inexpensive wine.

Montlouis The village of Montlouis, situated just opposite Vouvray on the other side of the Loire River, produces white wine that is very similar to the wines of Vouvray. Montlouis is not exported in quantity.

Provence

The vineyards of Provence are among the oldest in France. Phoenician traders entered Gaul by way of the Mediterranean Sea and were the first successfully to cultivate the vines that are now so much a part of life in this warm wine-making region.

The rosé is the most popular wine of the area, and it is fairly inexpensive. Prices will vary, but some very good Provençal rosés are available for less than $5.00. Provence produces some fine red and white wines in addition to the rosé, but they are not often found outside of France. The wise tourist will look for some of these inexpensive local wines when he or she visits the region.

Provence Vintages

The rosés of Provence should be drunk while they are very young.

Bandol   This area is entitled to its own controlled appellation and can produce red, white, and rosé wines. The red Bandol from the Domaine Tempier is one of the best wines of the district.

Bellet   The vineyards of Bellet, situated near the resort town of Nice, produce only a small amount of wine, which is consumed locally. Some very fine wines are made here, especially the whites and the rosés. The Château de Cremat makes an excellent white wine.

Cassis   The town of Cassis is located on the Mediterranean coast near Marseilles and is most famous for its excellent dry white wine. Cassis also produces red and rosé wines. It's traditional to drink the white wines of Cassis with bouillabaisse, the specialty of the district.

Côtes de Provence (The Slopes of Provence)   These
wines are of the VDQS and not the Appellation Contrôlée cat-

189

egory. Red, white, and rosés are produced under the name "Côtes de Provence," but the rosés will be found in greater quantity in this country. The Côtes de Provence rosés are very dry, fruity, and of good quality. Some particularly noteworthy examples of the Côtes de Provence rosé are Château Sainte Roseline, Château de Selle, Domaine des Féraud, Domaine de Mauvanne. The best wines of the region are entitled to use the words "Cru Classé" (Classified Growth) on the label, an indication that they are recognized as superior. The Côtes de Provence wines will soon join the ranks of the other Appellation Contrôlée wines.

Palette Château Simone is the most famous vineyard of this small wine-producing area. As in the other wine districts of Provence, red, white, and rosé wines are found here.

PART III
ENJOYING WINES

Serving Suggestions

In the traditional world of gastronomy, there are specific rules concerning the relationship between food and wine. Though I adhere to many of these rules myself, I must stress that they may be broken depending upon your personal preferences. Drink a bottle of wine *your* way, and do not be obsessed with rules. Above all, enjoy the wine and food experience.

The following guide merely suggests certain food and wine combinations that have been found to be harmonious. But note that wine should *not* accompany dishes containing oil and vinegar, i.e., salads, avocado with a vinaigrette sauce. Serve water instead.

White and rosé wines are to be served chilled, but not icy cold; two hours in the refrigerator is an adequate amount of time. Beaujolais can also be served *slightly* chilled.

Hearty red wine from Bordeaux, Burgundy, the Rhône Valley, and California should be served at room temperature, but this does not mean very warm: Try to keep your wine at a moderate temperature, between 60° and 70° F.

Cheese

Brie, Camembert, Munster, Pont L'Evêque, Reblochon, Port Salut	France: Red Bordeaux Red Burgundy Red Rhône Bouzy Rouge Gewurztraminer (suitable with stronger cheeses like Munster and Reblochow)
	California: Cabernet Sauvignon Merlot Pinot Noir
Chèvre	France: Sancerre Quincy Pouilly-Fumé Pouilly-Fuissé
	California: Sauvignon Blanc
Roquefort, Blue	France: Sauternes Châteauneuf-du-Pape Other full-bodied Rhône Valley wines Gewurztraminer

Chicken

Roast chicken	France: Red Bordeaux Red Burgundy Riesling Pouilly-Fumé
	California: Cabernet Sauvignon Pinot Noir

FOOD	WINE
Fried chicken, casual meals	France: Beaujolais
	Côtes de Provence Rosé
	Tavel Rosé
	Rosé d'Anjou
	Vouvray (Sec or Demi-Sec)
	Riesling
	Mâcon blanc
	Sancerre
	Brut Champagne
	Sylvaner
	California: Grenache Rosé
	Sauvignon Blanc
	Chardonnay
	Dry Chennin Blanc
	Johannisberg Riesling
	Pinot Blanc
	Natural or Brut Sparkling Wine
Veal roast, veal	France: Bouzy Rouge
	Red Burgundy
	Sancerre
	Pouilly-Fumé
	Pouilly-Fuissé
	Brut Champagne
	Riesling
	California: Pinot Noir
	Sauvignon Blanc
	Dry Chenin Blanc
	Natural or Brut Sparkling Wine

FOOD	WINE
Fish	France: Brut Champagne
	Corton-Charlemagne
(If a cream sauce accompanies	Chablis
the fish, a rich white	Meursault
Burgundy is most appropriate,	Montrachet
i.e., Corton-Charlemagne,	Pouilly-Fuissé
Montrachet, Meursault, etc.)	Pouilly-Fumé
	Sancerre
	Muscadet
	White Graves
	Riesling
	Sylvaner
	Gewurztraminer
	California: Chardonnay
	Sauvignon Blanc
	(Fumé Blanc)
	Natural or Brut
	Sparkling Wine
	Pinot Blanc
	Johannisberg
	Riesling
	Dry Chenin Blanc
Shellfish	France: Chablis
	Muscadet
	Brut Champagne
	Riesling
	Sylvaner
	California: Chardonnay
	Johannisberg
	Riesling
	Sauvignon Blanc
	(Fumé Blanc)
	Pinot Blanc
	Natural or Brut
	Sparkling Wine

FOOD	WINE
Game	France: Red Burgundy Red Bordeaux Pinot Gris
	California: Cabernet Sauvignon Zinfandel Pinot Noir
Roasts and steaks	France: Red Bordeaux Red Burgundy Châteauneuf-du-Pape Brut Champagne
	California: Cabernet Sauvignon Pinot Noir Zinfandel Natural or Brut Sparkling Wine
Choucroute (Sauerkraut, sausages, and ham)	France: Riesling Gewurztraminer
	California: Dry Johannisberg Riesling Sauvignon Blanc (Fumé Blanc)
	(Beer is also an appro- priate accompaniment to Choucroute)
Pâté de Foie Gras	
As an hors d'oeuvre	France: Sauternes Gewurztraminer Vouvray Demi-Sec or Doux Champagne Demi-Sec or Extra-Dry Pinot Gris

197

WINE

California: Sweet Semillon
             Sweet Chenin Blanc
             Sparkling Wine
             Demi-Sec

With the meal

France: Red Bordeaux
         Red Burgundy
         Red Rhône Valley

California: Cabernet Sauvignon
             Pinot Noir

Decanting

A bottle of red wine containing sediment (usually eight years and older), should be left standing upright for about two days prior to decanting. Since sediment is found throughout the bottle, it is necessary to separate it from the wine before drinking. This procedure coaxes the wine to the bottom of the bottle, enabling you to avoid mixing it with the wine when you decant. Decanting is the process of pouring wine from the bottle into a separate container called a wine decanter. This is done so that the wine will be sediment-free, and so that it may be given time to "breathe." All red wines, especially younger ones, need some contact with the air before being consumed. Exposing wine to the air will allow it to soften or mellow, making it much more pleasant to drink than if it had been served as soon as it was opened. To let your wine breathe, merely uncork the bottle about an hour before you wish to serve it (it is not necessary to decant a young wine that has no sediment).

When decanting does become necessary, watch the wine carefully and stop pouring once sediment begins to appear. Chances are you won't see a thing, even under good light: but one can assume that sediment will be found after three-fourths of the bottle has been poured. A very old bottle of wine (twenty years old or more) should be decanted just prior to serving. Older wines will lose their bouquet and flavor if exposed to the air for a lengthy period of time.

If you buy an older wine that has sediment, and do not have the time to stand the bottle upright for two days, you can always pour the wine into a decanter through a coffee filter or cheesecloth. This should only be done as a last resort, however, for the first method is far more desirable.

Trusting Your Wine Merchant

Choosing a good wine shop is not an easy task, but the consumer can be on the lookout for certain clues that can be used to deduce the quality, or lack of quality, of the store selling wine.

It has always been my policy to buy wine from a store that bills itself as a wine shop and not just a liquor store. The reason for this is simple: Most liquor stores are just that—establishments catering to the gin, whiskey, vodka, and scotch crowd. Chances are that if such a store carries wine, it does so only as a token gesture. Even shops that specialize in wine sell liquor; they must in order to compete. But in a wine shop, the hard stuff takes a back seat to wine. An important factor to consider is that a store selling mostly liquor will probably have neither a good selection of wine nor knowledgeable wine salespeople who can help you make a wise purchase. But a shop that concentrates on wine rather than liquor will be more likely to have a fine selection of French and California wines, as well as experienced salespeople who can intelligently discuss the subject of wine.

Knowing the names of different French and California wines is only the first step toward complete satisfaction. If your merchant is serious about his job and has made an attempt to study wine, he can provide you with supplementary advice concerning the bottle of wine that best suits your needs and your pocketbook. Only when a wine merchant is capable of giving sound advice of this kind will you feel satisfied with your purchase and encouraged to continue buying wine from that store. The wine enthusiast must have confidence in his or her merchant, but alas, few merchants are capable of inspiring such confidence.

Your merchant will reveal his or her qualifications in two ways: by the way he or she stores and displays wine and the way he or she talks to the customer about wine.

A wine shop must have adequate storage facilities. A good shop will have a temperature-controlled cellar (perferably a dark one), which keeps the wine at a relatively constant temperature throughout the year. Great fluctuations in temperature can ruin wine. If the proper temperature is not maintained in the cellar *and* in the display area, there is a good chance that the wine will spoil if it is left there for a prolonged period of time.

One can also discover a great deal about a merchant by observing the way in which that merchant displays wine. I am always very skeptical of a merchant's knowledge when I see that wine is stored on the shelf vertically instead of horizontally. A wine bottle should always be stored on its side so that the wine will moisten the cork, thereby preventing air from entering the bottle and enabling the cork to slide out of the bottle more easily when you are ready to open it. A cork will turn brittle and allow air to enter the bottle if it does not come into contact with the wine.

Another important point to remember is that wine should not be stored in direct sunlight. A merchant who places wine in front of a large display window, allowing the sun's rays to beam down on the bottles, is not taking proper care of the wine.

Even the inexperienced consumer will be able to recognize a good wine merchant when he or she hears one, because a good merchant is always talking to a customer about wine, and doing so with great fervor. It is virtually impossible to be in the business of selling fine wine without becoming emotionally involved. Good merchants speak of their wine collection with pride and love, like parents boasting of their children. A merchant must enjoy working with and studying wine if he or she is to act as a knowledgeable advisor to the consumer. More importantly, a good merchant is one who will *inspire* the purchaser to explore the world of wine. A merchant will not be in a position to do this unless he or she has a broad selection of *reasonably priced* wines from France, California, and other areas.

As I have tried to point out, there are many fine examples of inexpensive French and California wines, so beware of the merchant who tries to sell you a very expensive wine when you ask for suggestions. A novice to the field of wine should not pay exorbitant prices for a bottle that will probably not bring satisfaction in proportion to the amount of money spent. Neither a beginning wine student nor a seasoned taster need spend a great deal of money in order to enjoy wine. The greatest satisfaction comes from obtaining an inexpensive bottle of wine that tastes like a much more expensive one. For example, one can sometimes find an older vintage of a good Cru Bourgeois, or even a Fifth Growth, from Bordeaux for much less than one of the more famous higher-ranked growths. Your merchant should direct you to one of these wines, unless you specifically ask for something more expensive.

Let us not forget the many excellent values to be found among California wines. Remember, it is not necessary to spend more than $5.00 for a fine California varietal wine, or more than $2.00 or $3.00 for a good generic wine. If the merchant is not aware of these wine values, or does not have a good selection of reasonably priced French and California wines, that shop is to be avoided.

A serious merchant will attempt to establish a meaningful rapport with the customer. This means that the merchant should be willing to talk to you about your particular wine-buying problems, or about wine in general, whenever you are in the store. A salesperson who treats the customer as though he or she were unimportant and annoying does not deserve the time of day from a wine enthusiast. Patronize only those wine shops that have helpful, considerate, and knowledgeable salespeople. A salesperson obviously lacking in expertise is unable to make specific suggestions when you ask for them. Someone who points you to a section of the store and says, "Well, the French wines are here, and the California wines are over there," is remiss as a wine merchant. If you just want to browse through the store and take a look at the stock for yourself, you should be able to do so. A bad merchant will grimace and look dismayed when you say that you are there "just to browse." A good merchant welcomes the curious individual who shows an interest in exploring the nooks and crannies of the shop. Besides, anyone who takes the time to browse will eventually buy a bottle or two.

It is difficult indeed to find wine shops that meet all of the criteria I have set forth, especially in our impersonal, mass-produced, assembly-line society. But it is possible to find a shop that gives courteous, personal, and knowledgeable service if you make an effort to look for one. In my opinion it's worth the search, because half the fun of the wine experience is in the buying.

Index

211